The Old Man
and the Cat

The Old Man and the Cat

A Love Story

NILS UDDENBERG

**Translated from the Swedish
by Henning Koch**

THOMAS DUNNE BOOKS
ST. MARTIN'S PRESS ✿ NEW YORK

THOMAS DUNNE BOOKS.
An imprint of St. Martin's Press.

www.thomasdunnebooks.com
www.stmartins.com

Designed by Anna Gorovoy

The Library of Congress Cataloging-in-Publication Data is available
upon request.

ISBN 978-1-250-05975-8 (hardcover)
ISBN 978-1-4668-6508-2 (e-book)

First published in Sweden as *Gubbe Och Katt* by Natur & Kultur

First Edition: October 2015

10 9 8 7 6 5 4 3 2 1

To
Lotta, Daniel,
Samuel, and Elias for
making The Kitten possible!

The Old Man
and the Cat

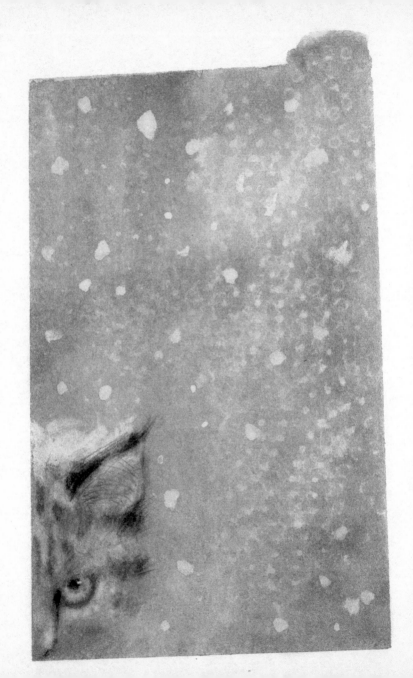

1

I am a qualified doctor; I am a lecturer in psychology and empirical, practical research into philosophies of life. The government has been kind enough to credit me by name of professor. But, for my own part, I am happy to call myself a writer: over the years I have published a large number of books, some of which have sold reasonably well. Nowadays I am also a cat owner or, I wonder, is it in fact the cat who owns me? Well, yes, that's probably the case—in real terms.

This is the story of how I "came down with cat," even though I had decided I would never, ever, own any pet. It's a banal story, maybe even a little ridiculous. But I'm in my seventies, and I have no status to defend and no career to fight for. I can allow myself the liberty of telling this tale. Like many older men I am fairly wet and sensitive. But the cat, as we'll soon see, has a will of steel; or maybe it is closer to the mark to say that she has a methodical, soft determination. There were never any confrontations, but in the long term that cat got what she wanted. This was how it started.

At the end of October, my wife and I came back from Namibia. I have always loved traveling and we have been to Africa before. We had driven a four-wheel drive for two weeks through the Namibian desert, visited large, empty national parks and seen elephant, zebra, and many elegant antelopes ranging the wilderness. Naturally we had also seen the obligatory big cats, the lions and leopards, but not so many of them on this occasion.

We live in a little house in the center of Lund. Our garden is surrounded by a wooden fence, which in most places is entirely covered in ivy. We park the car in a carport, and between the garden and the carport we have a gate that is always kept locked. This is immediately by our ground floor bedroom window and when, about a week after we had come home, I raised the blind to let in some pale autumn light, there was a cat sitting on the gate, looking at me with large, yellow eyes. She was a small, gray-brown speckled cat without any white markings. We had never seen her before, but we assumed that she lived in one of the nearby houses.

The little cat kept turning up in the days that followed, and before long we realized that she was spending her time in the little garden shed that is built onto the carport, with its entrance from the garden. A couple of times, while picking something up in the shed, the cat peered out from the basket where I kept some implements. We understood that she was spending the nights in the garden shed, where she got some shelter from wind, cold, and rain. Obviously, that morning when she unexpectedly showed up on the garden gate, she had been sleeping in my garden basket. She had made herself as comfortable as possible. The weather had turned cold and when, a few days later, we looked into the shed we saw that she had curled herself into a tight ball. She couldn't be especially comfortable; garden implements are not exactly bedfellows of choice. The only thing to provide a bit of comfort were my gardening gloves.

We went to the apartment we have in Stockholm and stayed away for almost two weeks. All the time I was hoping that the cat would realize that we were not a good bet, that she would understand that she had everything to gain by going home or finding some other protectors. But when we came back, the cat was still lying there in my gardening basket and watching us with her big, yellow eyes when we opened the door of the shed.

Winter came early that year; our unheated and

draughty garden shed can hardly have been a salubri-
ous place to spend the harsh winter nights. But the cat
seemed to be feeling well, both alert and in good physical shape, her fur thick and lustrous. But how in the
world was she getting by? Did she have some owner
somewhere in the vicinity, where she could go for some
food now and then, or . . . ?

There is something special about a cat's eyes. They
are large and face forward; like humans and other primates, cats have three-dimensional vision. Nor do
cats turn away their eyes; like small children, they just
stare right back at us. It is easy to start seeing an appeal,
maybe even reproach, in their gaze. In any case we were
overwhelmed by pity, we removed the hard gardening
implements and put an old worn-out beach towel in the
basket. Our son, who had visited us with his family a
few months before, had forgotten some of the dry food
that he gave his dogs. Maybe, we thought, cats eat dog
food. We put some of the dog food on a flowerpot sau-
cer and served it up outdoors; we didn't want to let the
cat inside the house. The cat smelled the food, guardedly at first, then she started eating greedily. Apparently
she was ravenous.

Again we went to Stockholm and once more we
were gone for almost two weeks. When we came back

it had snowed and I went to the shed to fetch a shovel, so I could clear the drift that had built up outside the car port. THE CAT WAS STILL THERE!

What could we do? While we were in Stockholm we had been talking quite a bit about the cat. We had been hoping she would leave on her own—we'd hardly been hospitable. Certainly she was a sweet and alert little cat and we had nothing against cats per se, but we often spent long periods in our apartment in Stockholm and we liked to travel. With our lifestyle we could not have a cat, it was just impossible. A cat needs to be able to depend on its hosts, and we were not dependable. The most likely thing, we consoled ourselves, was that she had got herself lost. Someone nearby was probably missing a gray-brown speckled kitty.

We put up notices. Someone from the next street responded, and wondered if his cat was causing us inconvenience. Not at all, we said, but maybe he was missing it? He wasn't. Obviously it was not his cat that had a habit of spending the nights in our garden shed. No one else expressed any interest, and we took down the notices. There we were, quite helpless, with a cat that had decided to live with us.

From time to time when we went to our grocery store we had seen posters appealing for donations to a community association that took care of homeless cats. They seemed to be feline-friendly, tender-hearted people well used to taking care of summer strays; maybe they could help us find a home for our little kitty? Oh yes, they could certainly understand our problem and they were pleased that we had turned to them, but their home for cats in distress was fullfull to bursting.

There was still the police. I called them. A friendly female voice answered, and I explained, a little bashfully, that I had no crime to report, only a silly question: "What do you do when a cat starts living in your garden?" I was hoping that someone had reported a missing cat to the police. My call was transferred and I spoke to yet another friendly lady, this one a police officer, who checked her register of missing cats. No one was looking for a cat like ours.

Continuing my conversation with the friendly policewoman, I admitted that we were finding it difficult resisting the cat's efforts to make contact. It just didn't feel right to let the stubbornly affectionate creature sleep out there in the freezing cold. The lady at the other end of the line was very understanding, maybe she even had a cat of her own. I couldn't tell. Of course, she explained, cats can be out of doors in winter—I knew that myself—but if it got too cold they sometimes got into trouble. Their ears and the tips of their tails could get frostbitten, and they needed sustenance to build up protection against the cold. Yes, I knew this, too.

But it just so happened, I explained, that I absolutely could not have a cat. How on earth should I deal with this? The most important thing, said the friendly lady, was never to give the cat any food. They're freeloaders, she explained, and if one gives them food they stay. I admitted slightly guiltily that we had been overcome by compassion for the persistently affectionate little creature, and we had given her food on one or two occasions. But, I added, as if to emphasize my firm principles, only ever outside. Which was true, more or less. Without any accusation in her voice, she suggested that this might be enough in itself. The cat already viewed us as a resource, which had to be maximized. I understood very well what she meant.

She said that the police could come and get the cat, on the condition that I managed to catch her. The police would bring the transport cage. I explained that catching the little animal was the least of problems, she sought contact with us as soon as we showed ourselves. I turned the question round: "What would the police do with the cat once they had her?" Well, said the understanding policewoman, they would bring the cat to an animal holding center that might be able to find someone willing to take care of her. At worst, they would have to put her down. I thought back on the animal tests I had run on cats when, during a period in my youth, I had worked as a teacher and trainer at the department of physiology, and did not ask any more about it. Instead I just thanked her for being helpful, and hung up.

Something inside me said, "No!" With her determined approaches the cat had shown a measure of faith in us, which I found it difficult to be unmoved by. To let the police take care of her would feel like a breach of trust. In that case, I thought to myself, I'd rather take the cat myself to the nearby animal hospital and pay for her to be put down as painlessly as possible. A good death would be better than a bad life. I had started taking responsibility for the cat's well-being.

We put out food, still outside. The cat ate and was allowed to sleep in the garden shed. In the beginning we only put out food now and then. But there was a lot of snow and it was properly cold, and our empathy grew. Lynxes and wildcats can cope with hard winters, I thought. But only if they get food. Our son's leftover dog food ran out and we tried offering the cat our own leavings: sausage, chicken, fish au gratin. Certainly the cat ate it all, but she was a little dubious about it. Before long we had bought a bag of dry food with a tuna aroma. I felt a little silly when I put the cat food on the conveyor in front of the familiar cashier in the grocery store. I wasn't someone who bought cat food, it was not a part of my self-image, and I felt a need to explain myself: "A little cat has moved into our garden shed and we feel sorry for her." "Well, then she'll probably stay," she explained. She sounded convinced about that, maybe she had some experience of her own to draw on. Of course she'll stay, I thought with a little sigh.

Kitty was over the moon when we came home with the new food. Obviously the pet food manufacturers know the sort of thing that tickles a cat's fancy. Food like that was also cheap, a bag lasted a long time and we made sure we always had cat food at home.

So gradually that it never actually happened, we began to view the little animal as a part of our daily lives. With a slight sense of surprise, I was able to confirm that the question, "Where's the cat?" had become one of our commonest phrases. Without at any point having made a decision about it, we had become cat owners.

But I was still not convinced that we, with our lifestyle, were suitable candidates for having a cat. Our daughter, who had met the cat on several occasions, came to our aid. We had familiarized her with our dilemma, and she told us frankly that she felt we were "suited to having a cat." We just felt good with that little animal running around us. Anyway, she had

also been charmed by our little Kitty and both her sons spoke enthusiastically about grandmother and grandfather's cat. Our son-in-law was very firm about it, he did not want a cat in their house. Our daughter, who's a social scientist and used to settling both practical and emotional problems for people, spoke the deciding words, "Can we have joint custody? I'll look after Kitty in those weeks when you're in Stockholm." The thing was decided. The cat could stay.

During the Christmas break I didn't have much reason to go to Stockholm, one and a half months elapsed without a single trip. Routines evolved. The cat—we still called her "our little Kitty"—still slept in the garden shed. Was it our hesitation about having a cat that made us treat her like that, or did we want to test her determination? Well, there could be no doubt of that. Every morning when we rolled up the blinds, the cat was sitting on the porch, in the snow, or even on the window ledge; at other times she came bolting down the path our grandchildren had shoveled from the garden shed to the house. They called it "Kitty's path." Already after a week, the cat materialized as soon as we touched the window latches. Had she been sitting there, waiting for us to wake up? Or did she hear when we started moving about and quickly got into position? A jump inside and then a brisk stroll into the kitchen to check if there was food and milk. There certainly was—indoors, nowadays.

On the odd occasion, the cat did not come running at once. To my surprise and irritation I noticed that I grew concerned. Where was she? Had something happened? Was she disappointed in us, had she abandoned us? It was not only the cat that had become attached to us, or rather to our garden and our house. We had also become attached to Kitty.

I loathe the winter. As a native of Skåne, I have never learned to do something fun with below-zero temperatures and snowdrifts. Skates and skis don't seem to fit my feet. I just find that the snow gets in my way and makes the streets impassable and slippery. Every snowy and dark winter's day is something to be endured— my mood is not always the best. People often try to console me by mentioning how the snow illuminates things. Yes, that's true, I suppose, but I wouldn't hesitate to choose darkness with freedom of movement. Maybe it sounds grumpy, but I honestly prefer misty, clement winter days to an ever-so-radiant sun on newly fallen snow.

Now the cat came to the rescue. There she sat one morning against the windowpane, as usual, looking at us with her big, round, yellow eyes. But to get inside, she had to either reverse or jump down into the snow again, then make another leap into the right window. She looked around, peered at the snow with distaste and chose to reverse. Walking backward on a narrow, snow-covered window ledge is not wholly easy, not even for a lithe little cat, and her maneuver looked so comical that I could not avoid laughing. Immediately, my surly winter morning mood picked up.

True enough, the cat had caused us a certain amount of worry, not least while we were trying to get rid of her, but it couldn't be denied that she had also given us a great deal of joy. If we help you survive the winter, I thought, you can help us, too.

As I said, plenty of snow fell that winter, and we had lots of it on our old roof, where after fifty years of service the asbestos tiles were starting to give up. After the cold and the snow, once the thaw set in, it started leaking. In an attempt to put an end to the misery, we put up ladders and tried to shovel the snow away. It was heavy work, the gutters were filled with hard ice, the drainpipe frozen up and covered in an impressive icicle. We shoveled and swore, but the cat was delighted. She loved climbing the ladders we were using to do our work. When we first noticed that the cat had climbed up on the roof, we wondered how she would manage to get down again. It went really well; calmly and carefully she placed her paws on the rungs of the ladder and made it down as elegantly as one could ever wish. My wife got her camera. How sweet she was, we said proudly. She was certainly both agile and smart enough to get herself out of a tight spot.

We were caught! Our resistance had been overthrown, or rather, gradually eroded. The cat had won. I think she knew all along that she would. Otherwise she would not have been so methodical and purposeful. My wife, and myself no less, have capitulated to her seductive arts.

A few of my contemporaries, male friends of mine, have fallen in love with new, often considerably younger women. It would be dishonest to deny that I have been tempted by the notion of one more time feeling a rush of love giving new youth to body and soul. But I don't have the energy and, apart from that, there's no reason for it. My wife and I are very much at home with each other; we have shared a long life. Losing her would be a greater loss than any compensation of a new infatuation. It is far better, in this case, to lose my heart in a small way—because I certainly have—to a cat.

Kitty engenders feelings of both tenderness and

interest. She has thrown in her lot with us and is absolutely faithful. My feelings for her surprise me. Like someone love-struck, events have been absolutely unexpected. The cat affects my life just enough. There's no need to get divorced, yet I can allow myself to get involved in a way that I would otherwise have said was beyond me. Our daughter says that Kitty perks me up, and there's some truth to that.

2

I have always been fascinated by animals, and as a boy I lived in a house where there was enough space for a small menagerie. I had an aquarium in my room, also a small terrarium with beetles, and also a considerably larger one with western green lizards, Greek terrapins, and a couple of grass snakes.

In addition I had two birdcages: one with budgerigars and another with zebra finches, goldfinches, and other small birds. At night I sometimes heard my mice clambering about in the curtains, when they wanted to get at the seeds, which we fed to the caged birds.

Most people would probably have disliked having mice in the bedroom at night, but I just found it homey. There was also a dog in the family—a black standard poodle—and a gray brown tabby cat: Kissicki. In time, Kissicki had a kitten with the same markings as her mother. We found her much more ungainly than her elegant mother, and so we named her Lumpy-Clump, although usually we just said Lumpy.

There was much work involved in taking care of all these animals. Taking the dog for walks was not so taxing, and I often had the company of my father or someone else. I have no memory of ever having to worry about dog or cat food. The aquarium fish were given dry fodder and on some odd occasion waterfleas, which we bought or caught in some pond. Bird seed was no great feat getting hold of either.

It was far worse with all the animals in the terrarium. The terrapins wanted fresh greens, but were often fussy eaters; the lizards appreciated fresh earthworms, which, with a bit of effort, one could dig up in the garden. Worst of all were the grass snakes; they wanted live food, preferably frogs. Usually I loved busying myself with my menagerie and I had a lot of good help from my sister. But there was a limit.

I was probably sixteen or seventeen years old when at some point in early autumn I made an irrevocable decision: the animals had to go. I wanted to rid myself of the responsibility, and I devoted a whole weekend to letting go of my menagerie. The grass snakes were no problem, one only had to release them in a suitable spot.

The beetles were a Swedish species, so they could go in the same way. The terrapins and green lizards were transferred into the care of a biology teacher with an interest in terrariums. He was probably concerned that they might have some disease, which would infect his own considerably more valuable animals, so at first he was a little reluctant. But he understood my need and in the end he allowed himself to be persuaded. What he did with my animals I do not know. The aquarium fish were left to "naturally depart," the blue gourami lived the longest. I seem to remember that the birds were moved into the room of my little sister, who had avian interests, and the dog and cats were on the whole the responsibility of the whole family, and also the most loved.

Whenever I have made crucial decisions in life— getting married and so on—they have tended to ar- rive successively. But this time I remember how it was suddenly absolutely clear to me that I would never again take responsibility for any household pets. I kept to that decision for almost sixty years. But now, Kitty lies in her basket in front of me by my desk and it reminds me of the cats when I was a boy, which were my constant companions while I was doing my homework. They liked to lie on the table under the desk lamp, it was warm and cozy there.

But although I had made an unshakable decision

never again to take responsibility for any pets, I did not relinquish my interest in animals. I carried on collecting beetles and watching birds. It was considerably easier than keeping animals of one's own. The beetles didn't ask a lot of me, stuck on the pins in my collection; wild birds are self-sufficient. I still recognize far more bugs than the average Swede, and whenever my wife and I have traveled hither and thither in the world, it has often been birds that have tempted us.

But also other animals, whether large or small, have interested us.

My character has probably been slightly formed by "the presence of cat." Kissicki—or was it Lumpy—used to lie in my bed at nights. That was probably after the birdcages, and therefore also the mice, had been moved. On one occasion I remember that one of the cats, probably the clumsier daughter, managed to slip into the bathtub when it was full of water. She was frightened and sopping wet, and after we had helped her out she ran into my room and burrowed between the top and bottom sheet of my bed. It was quite touching, but the bed had to be made up again after the sheets had dried.

On Saturday evenings, when I had no homework, I used to lie in bed listening to *The Carousel,* a very popular radio program introduced by Lennart Hyland, who later become the first television idol in our country. I had the cat in the bed with me, and it felt safe, warm, and cozy. So, as I was saying, I am probably slightly formed by "the presence of cat," and our current cat has exploited that—with utter ruthlessness.

Even after I became an adult, there were cats in my world. My mother, who became a widow in her fifties, always had both a dog and a cat. I think it gave her a feeling of security, and as she was not a sociable person, she liked having some movement around her. In fact, cats suited her best. Dogs wanted long walks, and that was never to my mother's liking. The cats were just there, and they caused her fewer problems.

But my mother's cats never felt as close to me as Kissicki and Lumpy, and the same could obviously be said of my sister's cats and dogs. I was happy to pet them and talk to them, also to talk about them for a while, but at the same time I thought to myself No, I'll never have a cat or a dog. I knew it with absolute certainty. And now here I am.

In time my mother became something of a cat fancier. Apart from her living pedigree cats—only one at a time—she had a collection of about a hundred cats in ceramic, porcelain, metal, and papier-mâché. Some of these were banalities from some flea market; she was often given cats as presents from children and grandchildren who did not know what to give her for Christmas or her birthday. Others were veritable works of art, which cost her a pretty penny to buy. I have kept a few of the latter and they have pride of place in the house where I now live. But most of my mother's cats have been scattered to the wind, so to speak. I have never bought any of those porcelain cats and I never will. I don't think I will, I should add, just to be on the safe side.

The beauty, timidity, and hunting instinct of the feline animal have always fascinated human beings; it has been a cherished motif for artists. My mother's colorful porcelain cats are mostly decorative. But other images of felines have had considerably more epic messages to convey.

Eastern despots of ancient times liked to have themselves depicted hunting lions. Elegant reliefs from Nineveh portray the king of kings, Ashurbanipal, standing in his chariot, an arrow in his tensile bow, while a hail of other arrows are already flying toward the escaping animal. In another image one sees the king thrusting his lance into a lioness's muscular body. The dying animal bares its predatory teeth, turns its head toward its pursuer, and roars with anger and pain. The entire scene is a celebration of the royal hunter, for anyone who can overcome such a wild animal must be a mighty human being. As heraldic animals, lions are unsurpassed. Countless crests and castle entrances are decorated with these big cats. Everything is very grandiose and boastfully masculine.

In ancient Egypt, possibly the original home of all domesticated cats, cats really counted, and they were more homely than the lions of the grand king. Admittedly the goddess Bastet, Baast, or Ubaste was originally a lioness, but over time she developed into more of a domesticated cat. One might think this a bit of a regressive career, but Bastet seems to have had a fond place in the hearts of the ancient Egyptians. There's a host of images and statues of her, and in some images she is surrounded by a litter of kittens. Cats have always had a reputation for fertility, and women who had not managed to get pregnant could, as a consequence, have every reason to confide in this goddess. Archaeologists have found hundreds of thousands of cat mummies in temples consecrated in her name. When the house cat died, the family was clearly capable of missing it, and if there was enough money to pay for it, the darling— or maybe one should say the protective goddess—was embalmed and buried in one of these "cat cemeteries."

There is something attractive about Egyptian cat culture. Cats are peaceful, down-to-earth animals that don't make much noise about themselves. And yet they have a certain gravitas. Even our little Kitty has something of the goddess about her when she purposefully settles into the most comfortable spot in the house. I certainly find it more possible to worship her than lion males, boastfully referenced by rulers across the ages, although on closer inspection they have proved to be lazy cowards, man-killers, even killers of their own cubs, who let the lionesses take care of the hunting and provide meat.

Of course the big cats are nerve-tingling: the lions, leopards, and tigers. A tiger that has developed a taste for human flesh is a symbol of all the cruelty that nature can express, and a roaring lion in the African night is a mighty experience. But my dream cat is of an altogether different ilk. It's the smallest of all the feline species and one of the rarest.

A female South African black-footed cat weighs about half as much as our little Kitty, who only weighs about six and half pounds herself. The male is a little bigger. Very few people have seen or even heard of black-footed cats and this very thing makes them even more stimulating to the imagination. "Black-feet" are nocturnal animals. They keep still in the daytime, but at night they sneak about in the expansive South African veldt hunting for voles, grasshoppers, scorpions and other edible things. They have had the common sense to keep away from humans and are firm individualists. Each and every one of these small animals has an extensive territory that is defended against all intruders. There is no question of any kind of communal life, as among lions. All attempts to tame the black-feet— and there have been many—have been in vain. These little cats may look as cute as you could ever wish, but they obstinately hold on to their solitary and predatory nature.

Sometimes I find our cat quite similar to a black-footed

cat. Her feet are black like theirs, and although black-footed cats have stronger markings, her coat is of more or less the same color as theirs. Sometimes I can't stop myself fantasizing that she may even have a bit of "black-foot blood" in her veins. Wouldn't it be exciting if she was half the size, yet retained all that natural feline wildness in her blood? Over the years I have seen many lions and I am happy about that, but a black-footed cat would be even more exciting and I am highly unlikely ever to see one.

Now that I have a cat and I am looking back at my life, I can recognize something that I have not fully been aware of up until now. Cats have always been *there* for me, and I have enjoyed them. It's as if they always knew that sooner or later I would fall for one of their seduction techniques. I grew up with a cat, both my sisters always had both dogs and cats, my son has two dogs, and my daughter is very happy to be Kitty's "backup mom". I am the one who defected. But it must have been written in my book of destiny that I would eventually "come down with cat"—that small household goddess with an independent spirit.

3

When sexing a cat one must make a close inspection. The male organs are not especially pronounced. In the early stages of our acquaintance with Kitty we were unsure if we were dealing with a tomcat or a queen. We were not so eager to have a tomcat, because uncastrated males sometimes have the unpleasant habit of marking out their territories, by spraying their really quite pungent urine on various things.

So we had a good look. It was exactly as we had suspected all along, our little Kitty was a female. In the period leading up to Christmas we even wondered if she was pregnant. She seemed a little curvaceous around the belly, and I gave a good deal of thought to what I would do if she produced a litter of adorable kittens. I'm far too much of a soft touch to separate a mother from her young, and have the poor little things put to death.

Still, I thought, maybe some local vet could kill them off in a more humane way. There was no way we could take on a whole litter of kittens; that was simply not on our radar.

But in the end there were no kittens, and we drew sighs of relief. As time passed, our little Kitty seemed to flatten out, if anything, around her belly, and in retrospect I have wondered if she had been suffering from dropsy. If one does not get enough proteins, fluids can leak into the surface tissue, giving the belly a round and almost traitorous appearance of well-being. One can see children with bellies like this in countries struck by famine, and our Kitty can't have enjoyed especially fat days while homeless in the harsh autumn and winter weather, before we properly took her into our care. It seems in bad taste, almost, to make a comparison like this, but human beings are made like this; we are moved by what we see in our immediate surroundings, while, for good or for ill, we have no problem closing our eyes to what is further removed from us.

After Christmas we began to see that the cat had us beaten. She had made her decision. She intended to stay and now it was for us to decide how we would handle the situation. One thing was absolutely certain:

we did not want any kittens. Giving a cat contraceptive pills seemed a fiddly task, especially a cat with such fixed ideas about food. All that remained was to have her neutered. We called a local vet. Surely it could not cost a fortune to neuter a female cat? The operation was set for a Monday morning in February.

Up until now, the cat had been spending her nights outside. We had a fantastical notion of her living partly as a farm cat and partly as a house cat. That way, we would keep more of our freedom. In other words she would continue to sleep in our garden shed. These days the basket was full of comfortable bedding and the weather was milder. She was not having too much of a torrid time out there. But then when it was time for her to go outside in the evening she grew less enthusiastic about it, and we had to keep the bedroom window closed to stop her immediately jumping back inside. As soon as we opened it in the morning she came running.

The night before she was neutered we kept her indoors. We had to keep track of her, and make sure that she was fasting before the operation. She had no objections about sleeping indoors. In the morning she was our usual perky cat, clambering all over the furniture and enjoying being stroked. She was even polite enough to jump up into the washbasin to pee. We put the cat carrier on the kitchen table. She had never been especially interested in it before, but this time she was. I walked out of the kitchen and, when I came back, she was already sitting inside it. All I had to do was close the lid, secure the latch, and lug it out to the car. And then we drove to the vet.

I had never been to a veterinarian's surgery before. The atmosphere was alien to me. People came in with big dogs, a few of which recognized where they were and seemed anxious, more or less like children waiting for their jabs from the school nurse. One of them was yapping disconsolately, another stood on the scales: just above one hundred pounds. Our own Kitty, who did not even weigh seven, looked very small indeed.

I really felt quite lost in this strange environment filled with loving owners, brochures about dog and cat insurance, and advice about how to keep your treasure slim and in a state of vigorous health. What was I doing there? Slowly it dawned on me that I was about to become a pet owner among other pet owners. What the heck was this blasted cat doing to me? And was this really what I wanted?

The vet is professionally friendly. I tell him that the cat was an orphan, and that we don't know where she's from. He explains that in view of this he must first examine her and make sure that she doesn't have a chip and isn't registered to another owner. If she is, he won't be able to perform the operation. I feel a little tense about this. I view her as our cat and I don't want her to end up with another owner. In fact it turns out that she doesn't have a chip, but now she must have one so that she can be registered as ours and be recognized as such, in case she is ever lost. And then she has to be vaccinated against cat plague and cat flu. It's going to cost about twenty dollars, but I don't protest about that. I just explain a little awkwardly that we and the cat are getting along quite well, and that she's sort of becoming our cat and I obviously want her to feel as good as she possibly can.

All the time there's a little thought chiming at the back of my mind: I'm not the type to have a pet. Can I really take the sort of responsibility that, it seems to me, a cat owner ought to be able to take? And yet here I am, as helplessly lost as a teenager with his first love. The vet asks what name we have for our cat, and I reply with a tentative air that we normally just call her "our little Kitty." And there it is, she has her name. It's entered into the veterinarian's journal: "Kitty," with a capital K, and so she is now formally registered to us.

After leaving Kitty there we go bird watching, and

one of the birds we see is a magnificent golden eagle. We have to do something. Just sitting at home waiting while the cat is being operated on wouldn't feel good. Bird watching feels safe and familiar.

We pick her up at about two in the afternoon. I pay and then we go to Granngården, a garden and pet center, to buy a litter tray and cat litter. Kitty has to stay indoors for at least a week now. She has a big cone around her neck, to stop her licking her wound, which would tend to keep it open and prone to infection. She is obviously bothered by the cone, but we're hoping that she'll get used to it and feel reasonable well in a few days.

When Kitty comes home she is still suffering the effects of the sedative. She limps about on crooked legs and vomits slightly a few times. One's empathy is awakened, along with feelings of guilt. She never asked for this, but it's a prerequisite for our continued co-existence. Toward evening she feels a bit better, jumping with some effort into the bedroom window, the one she usually relies on to get in and out, where she sits looking out into the darkness. Is she missing her basket out there in the coolness of the shed, is she missing the tomcats, who have been courting her from time to time these last few weeks? Or maybe she just wants to be in a familiar place.

In the evening I am tired—very tired. Yet I'm not the one who's been anaesthetized and had my belly opened up. The day has been so overwhelming that I almost feel slightly confused. I have become a registered cat owner; I am actually quite pleased about it. But I never ever made the decision to possess myself of a cat. All I have tried to do is handle the situation in which I found myself.

Maybe now it's time for a closer introduction of the animal now registered as a member of the family. Kitty is a small cat, as I said earlier her weight is less than seven pounds. The vet says that this is quite normal for a female cat, but as far as I'm concerned she seems much smaller than most cats I have met. In her gray-brown-speckled coat there are additional dark streaks, and although her fur is slightly fairer on her stomach, it is also gray.

When I go on the Internet to look into the matter more closely, I find out that she's a tabby, as all cats are called that have a pattern of patches or stripes in their fur. To be more precise about it, she's a mackerel tabby—in other words she has slightly curved darker streaks running along her flanks. The mackerel tabby is also known as the common tabby. These marking have a dominant tendency and will prevail even if only present on one side. For a cat to get a different coloring, the latter must be present in both parents. The explanation for this is very simple: mackerel tabbies look much the same as wildcats have done for thousands of years. Because, in fact, they are perfectly camouflaged.

Kitty's face is quite friendly, with large, forward-facing eyes. Some of the larger cats in the neighborhood—the tomcats, I like to tell myself—have longer, pointed snouts, but Kitty has a stub nose. She has strikingly large triangular ears and, at their tips, a pronounced tuft of black hair, almost giving her the appearance of a lynx. At the edge of her left ear she has a very slight injury, possibly from a cat fight, or maybe from one of her siblings when, as a little kitten, she competed for her mother's dugs.

Kitty has big paws and the hair between her toes is absolutely black. When she sits with her paws neatly together before her, there's a distinct black line between each toe. If she has any defect in her beauty it would be her tail, which is fairly short. She is far from being a Manx cat, they only have stumps for tails, but her tail could have been longer. Yet as far as she is concerned, her tail is perfectly adequate just as it is. She raises it up and wags the tip slightly coquettishly when setting off, or, when she is sitting, coils it decorously around her body. Sometimes she holds her tail in all four paws while elaborately licking the end. The upper side of her tail has markings in the form of five dark triangles.

The night after the operation, Kitty sleeps in our twin beds—for the first but not the last time, as we will soon find out. At some point in the night she makes her way onto a blanket on the floor. When I wake to go to the bathroom I almost trip over her, and I lift her back into the bed. She rummages about, and seeks

her way toward our heads. In the end I put my arm over her to hold her still. She pushes her nose against my cheek, gives me a little lick, and then closes her eyes. I have more difficulty settling down, when I turn around she wakes up again, coming to rest once more like a little furry parcel against my cheek. The horrible cone chafes against my cheek, but when I put my ear to the plastic I can hear that she's purring.

Why do cats purr? How do they do it? Do all felines purr? A purring tiger must sound like an electric drill being forced into a concrete wall. These questions are new to me, and I raise them with a friend who is knowledgeable about natural history. He passes on the question, and eventually I appear on a radio program with a professor of zoology, who patiently tries to answer my questions. At the end of the program she gives me a scientific article, in which a German scientist, very scrupulously and with many references to other researchers, presents everything science has to say about the purring of felines and other animals. Oh yes, there is fairly reliable evidence that certain other animals, for instance badgers, also have the ability to purr.

There is something wonderful about science. However trivial a question may seem, there is always someone who with the greatest possible seriousness has tried to clarify it with all the close scrutiny required by good science.

Cats, as science would have it, are possessed of little folds on their vocal cords. It is these that vibrate when they purr. And this purring takes place both during inhalation and exhalation, more or less as a violinist keeps playing both when the bow moves up and down. If one listens carefully, one can make out a little pause when the breathing changes from one direction to another. The purring is not just a sound; the entire cat vibrates.

This entire display of well-being, as we know, is very relaxed. But the fact is that purring does consume a certain amount of energy: the metabolism speeds up slightly when a cat purrs. Nature does not usually waste energy on irrelevancies, natural selection ensures this. So the purring must have a function.

The sound of a cat's purring does not carry very far, at most a few yards. The purring is a discreet sound, signaling closeness and intimacy. The same need for closeness is interesting when one considers the vibrations, which can only be best felt when there is direct bodily contact.

When we listen to a purring cat we feel relaxed and peaceful. The cat also seems to be feeling well, possibly even coquettishly twisting its body while we are stroking it. But no one would ever have stroked the African wild ancestors of the house cat, so purring can hardly be something for the delectation of humans. What about wild felines, when do they purr? Well, to a very large extent this is their secret. Purring is not a very noticeable behavioral trait, it takes place under cover and one has to get very close to a feline in order to hear whether it is purring. This is not always very easy. If the cat is of sufficient size it could even be dangerous. Not even the most dedicated researcher will sneak up to a tiger to check whether it is purring.

Nonetheless we do know some things: female cats apparently purr while mating. They also purr when giving birth, and this is more noteworthy. Although a cat generally has an easier time giving birth than her human counterpart, the delivery is hard work for her, and—as we have already said—purring does use a bit of energy. Kittens purr as soon as they enter the world. When the young are suckling, both they and their mother purr. The feline mother and her newborn kittens are united in a purring, gently vibrating universe of bodily heat and mutual presence. It actually seems quite cozy.

Humans like to think that a purring cat is signaling its well-being to us, more or less as when a person is walking along and humming to herself. This may be so, but the purring could also have a more specific purpose. When a cat purrs it may be an appeal for closeness, maybe even for empathy and help. There are accounts of injured animals purring while vets try to treat them, and this is hardly a comfortable, relaxed situation. Purring cats may be seeking intimacy, and it may not have been completely wrong when I felt flattered by Kitty pressing her horrible cone against my face in the night following her operation.

When she lies there in my bed beside my pillow I am happy that she is not a tiger. Tigers do not purr, apparently, nor do lions or leopards. But lynxes do purr, at least as adults; pumas purr, both the kittens and the adults. The same thing goes for the fleet-footed cheetah. Its purring is very loud, apparently audible at a distance of fifty yards. The status with the rare, elusive South African black-footed cat is unclear. But the photographs I have seen of it are so strikingly like our own house cat, that I assume it does indeed purr, and the most up-to-date scientific findings seem to agree.

A few days after the operation our little Kitty is depressed. I can't think of a better word for it. She shuffles about listlessly with the cone around her head. Won't eat or drink very much, tries half-heartedly to free herself of the cone, and sits on the windowsill looking out. Before, she always perked us up, but now when we look at her we only feel dispirited. She is a fragment of her earlier self—the joyful, agile, curious, and playful cat we have already learned to like.

But already by the third day after the operation she is more active. She looks around with energetic eyes and even manages to wriggle out of the cone. Full of happiness, she immediately starts licking her front paws and rubbing her face. Maybe, we think, one could remove the cone when she is eating, which is otherwise difficult with the cone in place. When she bends down to get to the food she pushes the plate away with its edge. We try to hold the food in front of her, but she finds it too elaborate. I am unused to being a sick nurse for a cat, but that is what I am and I have no choice about it.

Quite soon we find that Kitty is not the least concerned about her wound. She licks herself to keep her coat clean, but because the vet shaved off all her fur where he made the incision, there is nothing to lick there. We let her walk around without the cone for several hours, and soon she is back to her usual alert self.

She walks about the house, sits on the windowsill watching birds, starts playing with balls and nuts, and purrs, purrs, purrs. All three of us feel happier, and we decide to break the vet's orders.

Ten days later it's time for a checkup. In the last week she has generally been allowed to do without the cone, even though the vet told us she had to wear it for four-teen days. She has even been allowed into the garden in the mornings. We have kept an eye on the wound, which has healed nicely. There are only a few stitches that have to be removed.

The trip to the vet is a torment to her. It is not dif-ficult getting her into the cat carrier, but she doesn't like the car journey. Halfway there she starts meowing desperately. An odor of excrement fills the car. Kitty has crapped herself: there's a long turd on the blanket at the bottom of her carrier. Worst of all, she runs the risk of soiling herself, and that is one thing a cat doesn't like. Removing the stitches from the wound is a baga-telle, but on the way home it happens again. This time it's even messier, but somehow she manages to avoid filthifying herself. We let her out in the car—the police would probably not like that very much—and as soon as we arrive back home we carry her into the house. She wriggles as we go, but we hold onto her with a passive ferocity, we do not want her to run into the road in a panic. Once inside the house we let her go, and she immediately darts off to her favorite place at the foot end of my wife's bed, immediately next to my own. There, she curls up and goes to sleep. Only a few hours later she is ready to eat a little and start investigating the world.

After she has been spayed, it becomes a matter of routine for Kitty to sleep in our beds at night. When she had just been operated on, we could hardly let her sleep in the garden shed, and she gratefully cashed in on the improvement in comfort. Cats are prepared to put up with a great deal. But in choosing between what is okay and what's better, they opt for what's better. Certainly the warmth of the bedroom is preferable to a chilly night in March in our garden shed. So there she lies now, in my wife's bed. They are both really quite satisfied with that arrangement.

When in the morning Kitty comes up close to our faces, licks my cheek, and purrs, I think of the mother and her kittens, lying close together, purring, secure in their togetherness. Our spayed Kitty will never experience that. But I get the urge to purr back at Kitty and respond with the same comforting intimacy that she is showing me. I gurgle a little, but I lack those useful folds on my vocal cords, and it mainly sounds as if I am snoring. Nor does Kitty seem to understand my awkward attempts to imitate her comforting sounds. An area of our contact is out of reach.

4

Our little Kitty has gone. In the night she slept in my bed. I opened the window when I went to the bathroom at about four in the morning, and Kitty took her chance to go outside. An hour or so later she was back by our heads, sniffing at us and purring. This is how she has behaved lately, and we find it quite pleasant. We stroked her, but before long she decided to go out again, late night and dawn are her most active times. We fell asleep again and since then we have not seen her. It feels desolate.

Already when we were having breakfast in the garden I felt something was amiss. Kitty enjoys it when we are out of doors and likes to stay nearby, not in close proximity but close enough to keep an eye on us. But today she was not there, and when a little later I took a walk in the lovely spring weather, I could not quite enjoy the burgeoning flowers everywhere. Maybe, I thought, I'll never see Kitty again. As I write this a day later, she is still missing.

All day yesterday was defined by the sense of loss. The usual places where there used to be a cat, were empty. The cat food lay uneaten on the dish. Our son, daughter-in-law, and grandchildren who live in Stockholm had come to visit for Easter, then headed back at lunch-time. After they had gone, taking with them their "hundred-year-old" dogs, the emptiness felt even more pressing.

Aimlessly my wife and I walked round the block looking for our Kitty. But there was no sign of her. In the afternoon my sister and brother-in-law came to visit with their children and grandchildren. They were cheerful, talkative, and enthusiastic about our garden, which was at its very best, and yet the meeting ended up a little heavy. They had hoped to see our much-talked-about Kitty, but there was no cat to show off. After a few hours they left, and once again the feeling of emptiness descended.

When Kitty suddenly just disappears, it affects me more than I could have imagined. I am cut down by a sense of acute helplessness that I can hardly bear even to acknowledge. When the great tits make their three-tone calls, *titi-ta*, *titi-ta*, *titi-ta*, I have the notion that they are actually calling out, "Kittycat, Kittycat, Kitty-cat!" In the night both my wife and I dreamed that Kitty hopped in through the window, but it was just a dream, and when we opened the refrigerator in the morning to get out our breakfast, the tin of luxury cat food—tuna fish mousse—was in its place, opened, but without a cat to which one could offer the delicacy.

I try to remind myself that we have not actually known Kitty for very long. Yet, this little animal, although at first we tried to keep our distance, has obviously entered into our daily lives and become a part of a routine that relates very closely to a feeling of security. We may be concerned now about not seeing her for the past twenty-four hours, but just a few months ago we would have been more relieved than anything. Through this entire half-year period, Kitty has stirred up certain deep feelings that I am having problems dealing with. The emptiness in which I have wallowed for these past twenty-four hours is just another instance of it. It may be a bit ridiculous, but that is how it is.

I have lived a protected life, but like most others I have experienced sorrow on a couple of occasions. My father died far too early, and only a few weeks later we found out that we were expecting a child, who would have given him joy. When almost forty years later my mother stepped out of the mists of senility and sailed away into the brighter archipelago of memories that she left with us, it caused a combination of relief and sadness. The sorrow I felt when my parents passed away was both deeper and more overwhelming than I could ever feel about a cat. But such emotions are also more generally accepted, all people are prepared to take such things seriously. Missing a cat one has only known for six months, when it has only been missing for two days, seems the pathetic privilege of an old man. I have a wife, children, and grandchildren. I have friends and my writing that I find stimulating. Wake up! I can get myself another cat if I must have one.

But although I am wearily pacing about, wondering if I will ever see Kitty again, at the same time I cannot deny that it would be a relief if she disappeared out of my life. I never asked to have a cat, and now the cat has left. I have been freed from a responsibility. Maybe a happy love story is one where both parties thank each other for the time they have had, and then give each other the gift of freedom. Yet even as I try to console myself by thinking along these lines, the sense of loss is there the whole time—gnawing at me.

Naturally I am asking myself, why did she go? The dogs that came to visit could be a part of the explanation, but they are old, tired, and utterly harmless. In its youth, the smallest and fiercest of them loved to chase cats. But that was a long time ago, and now he lies half-blind and deaf, preferably curled up in his mistress's lap. The larger of them is about the most inoffensive thing one could find in the world, and really quite a coward—a couple of laps chasing rabbits are just fine for him, mainly because it is so wonderful just to run. But the idea of going after a cat—out of the question! When Kitty arches her back and hisses at him, he backs off at once. Of course, as far as Kitty was concerned there was no need at all for those dogs to be there. And if she ever comes back she won't miss them.

Probably the weather is a more likely explanation for her departure. When Kitty came to us it was quite horrendous: snowy, cold, and raking winds. The little bit of nurture we gave her must have felt good, maybe it was a question of life or death for her. Of course she had to keep hold of us under those circumstances.

But lately the weather has been wonderful and surely even a spayed queen can feel a bit of springtime exuberance. I mean, it has only been a few months since the sex glands and their secretions were removed. In recent days, Kitty has loved being outdoors. Like a teenager, she has only come inside to eat and sleep; jumping up to her bowl of food, and then, having eaten her fill, sitting in front of the door wanting to be let back out again.

Sometimes when she has come inside in the evening we have closed the window to keep her indoors. She has sat in the window, wistfully looking out for a few moments, then resignedly curling up in one of our beds and going to sleep. But the minute we've opened the bedroom window to let in the fresh air of the spring night, she has jumped outside.

Maybe she's been feeling imprisoned, and has now gone off to have her big adventure, wandering wherever her legs take her, where there is always something to discover for the one who does not concern herself about tomorrow. Right now the weather is wonderful for a cat, there is always somewhere to sleep and one can always do without food for a couple of days. Maybe she'll be back when her stomach is empty, and when the rain comes pouring down. Maybe then some human empathy will seem more attractive to her. This is how my fantasies go; they ease my sense of loss. She's feeling fine, she has left us of her own free will. Having said that, it was a bit impudent of her to just clear off after all our loving care.

The horrible feeling is that something could have happened to her. She loves exploring unknown nooks and crannies, she could have crept through an open cellar window that was later closed, or ended up in some other tight spot. Maybe she has eaten something that has made her sick? Or—what a terrible thought— another person could have adopted her as their house cat. She has no collar or other mark to indicate that she already belongs to someone. No one could possibly notice that little microchip in her neck, which the vet put in when he spayed her. Maybe someone has taken her or bribed her by offering softer beds and more delicacies than we did. In the faithless way of cats, she has chosen the best territory, the one with the most generous master and mistress. Now that we have given her both food and shelter, we feel she ought to be paying us back in "coziness services," but cats do not have a notion of such duties. Our identification with the cat, I feel, has been greater than hers with us.

When friends and relatives call to ask how our Easter weekend was, we've answered, "Oh fine, thanks, but Kitty has gone." Then they tried to cheer us up: cats are like that, they explain, not least in spring. They need their freedom and, just like Snufkin in the Moomins, they wander off aimlessly; after a while they come back as happy as when they first set off, making themselves at home as if nothing had happened. I thank them for their kind words, but I don't believe them.

When she has been gone two nights, we, or at least I, because I have a tendency to paint things black, feel quite sure that we'll never see our Kitty again. I put away her food bowls, they take up space on the kitchen counters and are painful to see. They make her absence so obvious. I want to throw away the cat food, too, but my wife stops me. Let's wait for a bit, she says, it may come in handy. And, as so often, she proves to be absolutely right.

On the third night Kitty turns up again. Just as we're going to sleep, we hear a familiar sound as she hops up to the window, and when I scan the bright spring sky I see her triangular ears and her short tail held aloft. Soon there's that little thud against the floor. "Kitty!" I call out to my wife, and quickly we're out of bed. We caress our Kitty—this is only moderately interesting to her—and then see to it that she gets some food, which on the other hand is exceedingly interesting. The food bowls are brought out again and are filled with the best the house has to offer. The milk is laced with cream. There is nothing halfhearted about Kitty's appetite. Cats are very reasonable creatures, whereas my emotional nature is something I am lumbering with.

We close the window. In fact it's far too warm to sleep with closed windows, but we don't want Kitty to think of leaving again, now that she's just come back. She quickly establishes that the exit is barred, but does not insist on going outside. Instead, she prioritizes contact with us. When I get up to go to the toilet she purrs and twists her body around my legs so insistently that I walk with difficulty. She clambers about in our beds; constantly seeking a way to get at our faces: headbutting, licking, and purring. From time to time she curls up and tries to go to sleep, but at the slightest movement she's up again. It's an unsettled night, but I think we're quite pleased, all three of us. Kitty is affectionate, but on her own terms.

In the morning we open the window. Kitty goes outside for a while but soon comes back. There's a cold northerly wind, so for the first time in a week we have breakfast indoors. Kitty jumps in and out of the window. Walks round, inspecting. Does she want to confirm to herself that the dogs have gone? What do I know?

Quite soon after Kitty disappeared we spoke to our daughter, who after all is Kitty's substitute caregiver. Like so many others, she said the problem would probably resolve itself once Kitty felt her stomach protesting and the weather getting worse. When the cat failed to come back on the third day she chose in spite of all to tell her sons that grandmother and grandfather's cat had disappeared. Both were upset. Their ten-year-old, Kitty's best friend, bravely suggested that sometimes cats go missing for a few days and then come back again. But in the evening he cried, because, like his grandfather, it comes all too easily to him to imagine the worst.

One does not call a family with young children when it's eleven o'clock at night to inform them that the cat has come home, but I give them a ring in the morning as soon as I feel they're up. My grandson answers and I tell him Kitty has come home. He's very happy, and I hear him call out, "Kitty's come back!" to his parents. He's just on his way to school, but we agree that he'll drop by as soon as his afternoon classes are done.

Later, our daughter tells us that the evening before he was praying to God to bring back Kitty. When he heard the telephone ringing in the morning, he said, "I hope that's granddad calling to tell us the cat's come back."

In the evening everything is just as it should be. Kitty is out for some air and comes in more or less as we are going to bed. She curls up on her mistress's bed and goes to sleep. To my mind, it's very comforting that she came back just as we had given up hope of ever seeing her again.

How can such a small creature, one that does not even weigh seven pounds, imbue me with such a sense of security? I am so much stronger, I could easily destroy her at any moment. She has no such power over me. Could it be the trust she shows me is what matters so much? I get to feel benevolent and friendly, and she gratefully accepts. Babies, similarly helpless, awaken similar feelings in their parents.

Many people invest large sums of money to acquire cats of exclusive breeding, Persian or Siamese cats or Russian Blues. Kitty feels like a gift. Quite unexpectedly she has become a part of our lives, and we've received her absolutely for free. Now that she has come back after going missing for a few days it feels better than ever. Cats do as they please, they have personal integrity and they choose according to their own desires. And—most likely without any kind of justification—we feel slightly proud to be the chosen ones.

Possibly Kitty has taught me a lesson. We have to trust her. I don't want a cat that does not stay of its own free will. If she prefers to be with us, she will stay, but if she wants to be elsewhere she will go. Her life has to be her own decision, all we can do is show her as much good-will as we can, and in this way demonstrate our desire to keep her with us. It sounds reasonable enough, but as one knows all too well it is not reason that holds sway. It is difficult for me not to be controlling, not to check on her whereabouts. We put a collar with an ID tag on her. Admittedly she is prettier without it, but we want it to be obvious that she belongs to someone.

On the radio I hear Jane Goodall say that she loves chimpanzees, but that the chimpanzees, even the ones she has grown close to, do not love her back. At most they trust her. Whenever this happens she feels proud and satisfied, as if shown a great honor. It's exactly like that with Kitty, I think, we love her but she does not love us back.

Slowly she has started trusting us, but we do not trust

her quite as much. One fine day she could be gone and we'll be left here with our loss and the refrigerator full of her delicacies. But at this moment I am just glad to have her back.

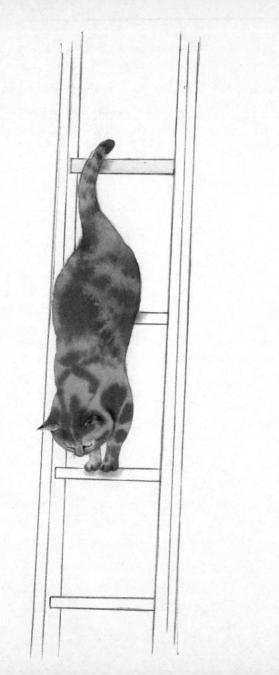

5

Kitty loves to play, and the games are always hunting games. Usually we weed the flowerbeds in spring. For instance, we remove old seed cases, which have been left through the winter so the birds can get at any seeds that may still be inside. The winter stalks of globe thistles are quite tall, with seed cases like little balls at the top. Kitty loves them. She wants me to hold them by their stalk, dragging the seed case along the ground so she can give chase. All I need do to make her spring into action, is stand in one spot and spin the globe thistle around me in circles. Kitty gets lots of decent exercise, while I mostly just get giddy. These kinds of hunting sallies usually end up with Kitty making a somersault as she lunges at her prey. It looks so comical that I burst out laughing. But Kitty does not feel

ridiculed, she just calmly lies there chewing her van-
quished seed case.

Through the winter the weather has often been
dull—wind and rain, occasionally mixed with sleet.
Cats and humans have reasonably similar views on
weather, what we dislike is also not greatly to Kitty's
taste. Dog owners have to walk their dogs however
pitiful the weather, which is probably good for their
health, but Kitty and I are rather comfortable by nature,
and we stay inside in the warmth of the house. Kitty
mainly sleeps and now and then makes little assaults on
the edge of some rug or any other thing suitable as out-
let for her energy. I get the idea that she is quite simply
having a boring time, but I'm not altogether sure that
cats can be bored.

When I come into our living room, Kitty often
climbs onto the back of an upholstered chair, and gives
me a demanding look. Her whole posture tells me that,
in her view, it's high time for something to happen. On
the floor lies a piece of wool, crocheted by one of our
grandchildren using a finger as a crochet needle. It
is multicolored and was made for the sole purpose of
being a cat's plaything.

I pick up one end and pull the other slowly across the
floor. Kitty gets into position, every muscle taut and

ready for the killing leap, her eyes attentively following every move made by the tuft of wool. Often she does not attack her prey until just before it disappears out of view. The victim must not get away. With marvelous precision she grips the flimsy bit of wool with both paws. And holds it very firmly. Sometimes she throws herself on her back, thus also freeing up her back paws. All four paws grip that poor, defenseless bit of wool. Her ears are slicked back, her predator's teeth tear at the wool and her facial expression is absolutely murderous. By now, our little domestic tiger is on a roll. We find her irresistible.

It is even funnier when one swings the thread in front of her and her head turns back and forth like a spectator at a tennis match. When the dangling piece of wool comes close enough she lashes out with her paw and almost always manages to catch it. If she can't reach it from where she's sitting, she tends to spring. It's more complicated but she's often successful and there is a great deal of satisfaction in the way she pulls down her haul and sinks her teeth into it.

Climbing is the most entertaining thing of all, Kitty feels. When we open the kitchen door she runs into the garden and reaches up against a tree trunk, where she sharpens her claws. If I approach her at this moment, she very quickly climbs the tree and, once she is high enough, looks down at me. It's as if she would like to call out, "You can't catch me, you can't catch me, you can't catch me. . . ." Her triumph is absolute and I get the notion that she relishes the feeling of her own agility and strength.

At the far end of the garden are some tall elder bushes, at the very top of which a pair of magpies have built a nest. Kitty likes to climb to the top, but decides fairly rapidly to come back down again. Not because she is afraid of heights—she doesn't know the meaning of vertigo—but because the magpies make such a dreadful noise and, in the end, get a little too invasive for her liking. A few times the magpies have also gained "supporting fire" from a couple of crows and then we have heard Kitty meowing a little disconsolately before opting for retreat. I mean, the birds are the same size as she is, and they have all the advantages on their side.

We have all heard stories of cats climbing into trees and needing assistance from the fire brigade to get back down. We look up nervously and wonder how Kitty's adventure is going to end. But she makes her way down as elegantly as anyone could wish, if not quite as rapidly as when she went up. Calmly and methodically she jumps from branch to branch, now and then stopping and looking around, as if assessing which route to take. Then she makes her decision and soon enough she is back on the ground.

As summer nears it is time to exchange the old, leaky asbestos roof for a new corrugated metal one. The construction company puts up scaffolding around the house and lays ladders on the roof, on which the roofers can climb. Kitty finds all this an excellent idea. It's an absolute cakewalk for her to make her way up to the ridge of the roof, balancing along it and jumping two feet onto the neighbor's roof before continuing toward their chimney. There she sits like a church weathercock, looking around. Higher than this she can't go. After a while she wanders back again, the same route but in the opposite direction. She seems to do all this for no other reason than that she finds it amusing. At least I can't think of another reason, and I can definitely understand where she is coming from. As a boy I loved climbing trees.

Sometimes the games turn rougher. It might all begin with my scratching Kitty's stomach. She twists coquettishly and purrs loudly. But after a while she puts four sharp paws and mouthful of needle-sharp teeth into my hand, which I am protecting with a thick glove, so that I can spin her round, round, while her attack on my hand intensifies. She continues purring throughout, at least until she gets too busy attacking me.

After a while she tires of this and hops aside, preens herself a little and tries to look unconcerned. "Don't imagine you can handle me any old way you like." But after another minute or so it's time again. I make a little movement toward her with my gloved hand, she responds by charging me, and the playful bout resumes. It all reminds me of when a mother makes playful lunges at her baby, who, with equal amounts of delight and shock, chokes up with laughter. The question is who enjoys it the most, the mother or the child?

"When I play with my cat," writes the spiritual father of all essayists, Michel de Montaigne, "who knows if I am not more amusing to her than she is to me." This French nobleman sat in his château at the end of the 1500s and let his thoughts run, more or less as I am doing at my computer in this moment. He wrote sinuous texts, in which the logic is not always evident, yet on the other hand there are frequent flashes of spiritual and well-articulated thoughts. When he referred to his writings as essays—*attempts*—it was exactly this explorative way of examining his own, inner world that he was referring to. And while he obviously felt that his thoughts were worthy of being written down and, further, of even being published, his manner is modest, almost timid. Montaigne never proselytizes. He asks questions of himself and his reader, and this soft-spoken mode of address is often more effective than bombastic proclamations.

What, for instance, is the relationship between animals and humans? Who can know, Montaigne wonders, what animals feel and think? Man, "born to so much misery," "haughtily" puts himself on an equal footing to God. And in an expression of the same conceitedness, he gives other living creatures "a measure of abilities and powers that he finds to be for the general good." But how can humans, with their limited "powers of reason" understand anything of what is happening inside the head of an animal? When comparing themselves with animals, humans always use themselves as a yardstick and conclude that animals are "stupid." Yet, Montaigne asks himself, can one really reason in such a way? It is difficult to get any further from the idiotic assertion of the philosophical genius Descartes, that animals are no more than marvelous machines riveted together by God, the super-engineer. I share Montaigne's uncertainty about what his cat thinks and feels while he is playing. Doubt—not certainty—is perhaps humanity's preeminent intellectual characteristic. The inner life of animals is a mystery to us and one of the many reasons why it is so exciting to try to spend one's time with them. Perhaps one should not be so sure, but I doubt whether a cat can feel doubt. In the noble art of questioning what we really know, humans are probably infinitely superior to all other living beings.

A cat's brain only weighs a fraction of its human counterpart—but it is still a wondrous miracle. It steers Kitty's paws when, with unfailing precision, they catch the wisp of wool that I dangle in front of her nose; it helps her keep her balance when she trips along the narrow banister around the deep well where the stairs connect the lower and upper floors in our house. And obviously it is also Kitty's brain that makes her purr as she coils around our legs when she feels it's time for a bit of food. A cat brain may not be equal to dreaming up far-reaching plans for the future, but it can definitely get an overview of a situation and prepare a highly successful short-term strategy. With the help of its little brain, our Kitty can persuade master and mistress both to serve up some food and trail a wisp of wool around.

Of course Montaigne was right. He was not unique in amusing himself with the cat, the cat amused itself just as much with him. I laugh at my Kitty whenever I find her sweet and cute. Cats can't laugh, but perhaps Kitty finds it entertaining, when all is said and done, watching me dodging about with my wisp of wool; maybe she smiles in a slightly superior manner when she notices how giddy I become after spinning around with the seed case of a globe thistle in the garden: "Humans are so clumsy!" I imagine that I am stimulating her hunting instincts when I play with her more or less as I played with my grandchildren when they were small. But with the same justification one could probably maintain that she has stimulated my "grandfatherly instincts." When it comes to the crunch, maybe we both socialize with each other on fairly equal terms. We are both captives of our own inclinations and maybe for this very reason we manage to establish a form of contact.

The cat's requirements and mine are very different. Our perceptions of what is happening, if a cat can have any such perceptions, are probably completely different. But we spend time together, Kitty and I, and we both enjoy it a good deal. Sometimes I grow tired of the game before Kitty does, but just as often she tires before I do. We go up to my study. I sit in front of the computer and she jumps up into her basket and looks out of the window for a while before she starts preening herself, then curls up into a sumptuously relaxed "cat pretzel."

We both feel fine and even if we don't understand one another, because we probably don't, one could say this is also a way of coexisting. I often think human togetherness occurs on the same terms. Two people believe that they understand one another, whereas in actual fact they are living on two different planets. Yet it can work quite well, at least for a time.

In the very moment of my writing this, Kitty is lying in her basket, two feet from the computer. Her head is burrowed deep into the towel; her tail hangs a fraction of an inch over the edge of the basket. I get a bit of company, but nothing that disrupts me as I try to concentrate on my texts. She gets a comfortable basket to lie in and a window to look out of, if she so wishes, while a radiator immediately under the basket spreads a pleasant warmth. And, like me, she gets a bit of company but nothing too disruptive. Again, we are both satisfied with the situation. Maybe this is what is known as friendship.

I don't know if Montaigne had his cat with him for company while he was writing his essays, but I'd like to think so. And I am almost sure that he would have appreciated it. As indeed the cat would probably also have done.

6

In one of his most well-known poems, brilliantly translated into Swedish by Britt G. Hallqvist, the Nobel Prize–winning poet T. S. Eliot claims that a cat must have three names: one everyday name, one that is more individualized and more personal, and one that only the cat is familiar with. The poet sighs. The naming of a cat is not something any old person can hit on the nail. I can only agree. Doris Lessing, another Nobel Prize–winner with a love of cats, has several names for each and shifts from one to the other depending on need. Sometimes she comes up with an entirely new name when she feels the situation demands it. Lessing's denominations are very loving; just like a baby, her kittycat acquires many nicknames.

Both Lessing's and Eliot's view of cat names exude a certain amount of insecurity. Eliot suggests that every cat has a name that no human could ever know, whereas Lessing's darlings change their names according to their, or their owner's, mood.

Our cat has now been a member of our family for more than a year, but she still has no other name than Kitty. Our grandchild, who is "Kitty's best friend," has suggested Naughty. And why not? The cat likes to lie in ambush behind a plant or a tall perennial in the garden. She is capable of turning up in the most unexpected places, when one least expects it. When we are sitting, reading, in the outside seating area under the corrugated plastic roof, there comes a sound of paws overhead. Kitty has got up there without our noticing. Naughty would be a good name in the spirit of Doris Lessing, maybe complemented with Sleepy when she spends an entire rainy day lazing about in one of her usual spots, my wife's bed or the basket near my computer.

But I think my own preferences lean more toward T. S. Eliot's naming etiquette, it seems more respectful than Lessing's innumerable baby names. Anyway, Britt G. Hallqvist's translation into Swedish of Eliot's poem is so instantaneously convincing. Rarely has nonsense poetry had such rhetorical power. So I imagine that our cat has a normal name, a deeply personal name, a name

I am at liberty only to fantasize about. The latter name is the one that most fascinates me, because it denotes what I can never touch in my cat, for the simple reason that I am a human being and she is a cat and the worlds we live in are infinitely different.

So, as a first name she could continue to be known as Kitty. It's caressing and friendly without being silly about it. Just like Nils, Lars, or Gunilla it is connected to the individual, not to a certain situation or behavior as in Naughty or Sleepy. Possibly it's slightly anonymous. All cats have at some time been addressed as Kitty, if for no other reason than because someone does not know their names yet nonetheless wants to make contact with them. Given that we have not got further in our name-giving, I fear that this could be a sign that we have not yet properly identified ourselves as cat owners.

In any case I am not sure she would respond to any name, whatever it was. Sometimes she seems to know that we are talking about her, but it's probably mainly the situation and our tone of voice that she reacts to. Whether we speak her name or not hardly seems to make any difference.

If we open the kitchen door and call out "Kitty," she does occasionally come running from some corner of the garden, but really I think it's more the fact that we are opening the door and showing ourselves that counts, it reminds her that she can come inside, have a bit of food, play or take a nap. It may sound as if I am indifferent to my cat's feelings, but I really don't think she cares very much about what name we call her by. So for the time being, Kitty will have to do.

Eliot's solemn middle names feel like a challenge. The Nobel Prize–winner puts forward a series of original suggestions, which are quite inimitable—no one else could ever have the notion of giving another cat a name such as, for instance, Jellylorum. Sometimes these names have a ringing note of blue blood or learning.

I am not a stranger to thinking along the same lines myself. Why not call our cat Aspasia, as in the fair and intelligent female friend of Pericles, the enlightened Athenian dictator? It would also be a name that hinted at both the cat owner's education, and the cat's influence over him. Aspasia did not lack power. There was gossip: certainly Pericles ruled over Athens, but in turn Aspasia ruled over Pericles. Aspasia is a beautiful name; it contains, as a cat's name should, a couple of hissing s sounds. It alludes to some of the philosophical wisdom of life that I would like to ascribe to our cat. But the intellectual life of this classical courtesan must have been a good deal richer and her love affairs considerably more sophisticated than those of our little spayed kittycat. So maybe it would be a bit over the top. Anyway, I wonder how the neighbors would react if I stood in the garden calling out, "Aspasia, Aspasia!"

I can only fantasize about Kitty's third, most secret name. It's as hidden to me as those thoughts—if a cat has thoughts—moving behind those big, yellow eyes now watching me so attentively; or those dreams, if a cat has dreams, that make her thrash in her sleep, twitches her whiskers, and stretch herself a little, before going back to the inscrutable nirvana of all cats.

So until now our cat has no other name than Kitty. Maybe she will never be known by any other name. Maybe this namelessness expresses something as significant as T. S. Eliot's third cat name. That she has a name of this kind I know for certain, although I obviously don't know what it is.

At this time in the summer Lund is vacated by the students, and the professors make their way from the university to their summer houses on the west coast or in Österlen. But many cats stay on in town and Kitty enjoys an intense period of nightlife. She sleeps all day and wakes up around six or seven in the evening and stays out of sight until the early hours, when she hops in through our bedroom window.

The summer nights are the enchanted time for all cats, it's almost as if they have the ability to go back to the first home of all house cats, in Africa. Admittedly the nights are shorter and lighter in the Nordic region than closer to the equator, but it is pleasantly warm. Insects, fledglings, mice, and other cats move about in the gloom. Occasionally we have even seen a hedgehog.

A cat's life is being lived around us, a cat's life that only in the odd glimmering moment touches our own lives. Unknown cats are sneaking about in the bushes. Tomcats emerge in the night, and sometimes they sit meowing a little provocatively in front of the kitchen door. Our little spayed queen cat is only moderately interested, often she prefers to jump inside at the window and stay out of the way, then go and investigate a little later. Usually the would-be suitor slips away after a while, the vegetation closes behind him, and he is gone as invisibly as when he came.

One of these toms is a black cat with a red collar, who comes strolling across the garden. He behaves quite discreetly, with an almost aristocratic superiority. It's as if our garden does not greatly interest him, he is on his way to other, more pressing destinations. Other tom-cats make more fleeting appearances.

All our temporary visitors run away as soon as we show ourselves in the window. While they are gallivanting about in our garden they are wildcats, but home with their families they are very likely cuddly kitties, lying on their mistress's lap and purring. T. S. Eliot is right, cats live a double life. The summer nights are their time; that is when they wrap themselves in their most secret cat-names and go out adventuring.

From a cat's perspective our garden is certainly a territory worth defending. Not just Kitty but other cats, too, seem interested. One of the latter is "the big tabby." He is much heavier than our little Kitty, and when he comes stealing out of the darkness in the evening we find him rather thievish. He often meows loudly, almost as if saying, "This is where I live." Guardedly curious, Kitty walks toward him but does not attack. In fact she is a little afraid. On one occasion we even wondered if she was raped. A terrific amount of meowing ended with our little Kitty rushing in through the kitchen door. She looked afraid, and when we went outside to investigate what had happened, the big tabby was standing there, marking territory by spraying urine at our doorpost.

Whenever we see the tabby we shoo him away. Kitty runs after him, as if trying to convince herself that in actual fact she is chasing the other cat off the premises. Probably the tabby does not have as much respect for her as he does for us, but it's good to feel that Kitty seems convinced we are on her side.

One early summer morning we opened the window and expected Kitty to come jumping inside, as is her habit. But no such thing happened! Instead we heard a terrible meowing, now and then erupting into furious hissing. Clearly there was a face-off somewhere nearby, between two cats. We called for Kitty, but nothing happened. The enraged meowing went on as before. When we went into the garden to investigate, we found tufts of cat hair in a few places. There had obviously been some rough stuff going on here. The tufts had more or less the same color as Kitty's coat. We walked around the block calling for her. My wife caught a glimpse of what could have been Kitty in a neighboring garden, behind a locked gate. There was nothing else to be seen, neither Kitty nor any other cat, yet we could still hear the odd irate yowl.

After a while the cat spat abated and blackbird song took over. But we were worried. Was Kitty hurt? For half an hour we were unsure of what had happened to her, but then she came loafing along with her tail in the air, as blithe as ever. Nothing about her suggested

she was the least bit hurt. Relieved, we stood ready to give her our choicest morsels. Kitty was not particularly interested—something else was stirring in her little skull Alert, she walked around the house and garden, as if wanting to assure herself that we were here and she still had the situation under control. Her food, although it was the best the house had to offer, was left untouched. After a while she curled up and went to sleep.

Where she had been we never found out. Had she been involved in the fight, or, like a princess in a fairy tale, watched as two knights settled their differences? Something important had happened in her cat world, at least we were sure about that. Although it had affected her strongly, exactly what had happened was her secret. What our ears had heard and our eyes had seen were merely a surface, beyond which there lay some murky cat experience that we could only speculate about. Of course I liked to think that she had been the princess, who had let the guys settle things between the two of them, but I couldn't rule out that she had defended her territory from an intruder. In which case she had made a good job of it: there was not a scratch to be seen on her, and all those tufts of cat fur could hardly have come from her.

Cats have difficulties understanding the idea of title deeds. Our territory and Kitty's are not the same. We feel she ought to be able to keep to our garden. There, she has bushes and trees to climb, tall perennials to hide behind, a birdbath with refreshing drinking water—imbued with a light aroma of blackbird—and the possibility of hunting both insects and mice. What more can a cat ask for? But for a cat, a hole in the fence large enough to crawl through is more important than the purpose of the fence, which is to divide one thing from another. The scruffy neighboring plot at the back of our land is probably at least as interesting to a cat as our own somewhat tidier garden. There are exciting things to explore everywhere.

Sometimes she crosses the road, where a building, once a retirement home, has now mainly been converted into local government office buildings. What interests Kitty are the bushes and all the nooks and crannies. We are less delighted about it. The road in front of our house sometimes has many cars on it, and we don't want her hurt. But we have no power over her. I know that there are risks attached to letting her run loose, but I don't want to keep her indoors all the time.

A cat can be the tamest of the tame, a homely purring sofa decoration allowing itself to be stroked by the children, and having no problem with being its master and mistress's spoiled baby. But the cozy day-to-day pussycat has another side; it is also a nocturnal, stalking animal of prey, cast in the same mold as the tiger or the leopard. It is this duality that has given cats the reputation of duplicity; hence T. S. Eliot's belief that a cat needs three names, including one that is "nocturnal, cat-like and 'always unknowable' by humans." The "tiger name," is of no great importance in the sofa but crucial during the nightly expeditions when the predator must take what it needs.

7

Near the latter part of the summer we have a cat flap installed in the kitchen door, big enough for cats and very small dogs, but far too small for even a well-fed Pekinese to get through. The cat flap is yet one more expression of the power Kitty has come to exert over our lives. A gap in the door covered only by a thin plastic gate obviously gives rise to floor-drafts, heat loss, and higher heating bills, but not as much as we had feared. Yet a portal of this kind is practical both for Kitty and us. Let me explain.

We go to Stockholm quite often; often I go by myself, at other times my wife, and occasionally both of us at the same time. Before, it used to be a problem. Kitty needed food and our daughter could see to that. But if we were gone for a week we could hardly keep Kitty locked up inside the house, so we used to move her basket into the garden shed, where, to the great pleasure of all the neighborhood cats, her food was also served. Apparently the big tabby made his presence especially known. When we came home and started giving her food inside again, we saw him sneaking into the shed in the hope of getting himself a morsel, only to come out a minute or so later with an air of disappointment about him. At least that is how it seemed to us.

A cat flap makes the whole thing a good deal simpler. The food can be left in its usual place in the kitchen and Kitty can sleep in her basket or on her mistress's bed. Not even a cheeky tomcat likes to enter an unknown house, especially one that is defended by another cat, if only a small female. With the help of the cat flap, we hope, we won't have any uninvited guests, and Kitty can come and go as she pleases while we are away. This is important, not least now as autumn draws near.

The reason for installing the cat flap at this particular time is that we are going to Africa. We won't be away for very long, but all those who usually take care of Kitty—my wife, our daughter, and our four grandchildren—are accompanying us. Our grandchildren have seen our photos of the large African animals and for a long time I have been promising to treat them to a journey, so they can also meet the elephants, rhinoceroses, hippopotamuses, lions, leopards, and all the other exciting animals and birds. Our son-in-law is staying home to work and he has promised to take care of Kitty while we are away. His task becomes a good deal simpler if there is a cat-flap; then he only needs to come to the house now and then to ensure that there is food in the bowls. Unlike my wife and myself, he is good with his hands. He has promised to install the cat flap well before we leave, so that Kitty has time to get accustomed to it.

Standing inside the store where they sell all kinds of accessories for pets, I once again have that feeling of being in the wrong place. What am I really doing here? The whole cat flap market seems a bit of a science in its own right. There are simpler models by several manufacturers: German, English, and French. Then there are certain models where the cat must wear a little magnet on its collar in order to get inside; this, for instance, would ensure that there were no unwanted visits by the tabby cat. But at the same time it seems a little complicated, and what would happen if our little Kitty lost her magnet? That would seem quite feasible, and in that case she'd be locked out. The most advanced models of all are the electronic cat flaps that scan the microchips worn by all respectable cats including ours—surgically inserted beneath the skin of their necks almost like identity documents. Kitty can hardly lose her chip, but would such a thing really work and how would one know when to change the battery required for the electronics? Technical wonders of this kind also cost a pretty penny. I stand there like the father of a newborn shopping for a baby carriage. Of course I'm prepared to pay for the best solution, but the sheer scale of choice here makes me confused.

In the end we opt for the simplest model, not because it's the cheapest but because it seems most reliable. We are counting on the tabby cat keeping his distance despite the absence of a magnetic lock. Installing the cat flap does not prove to be entirely simple. The door is thicker than the German manufacturer has estimated, and our son-in-law has to put in several shifts while we go back to the store for spare parts. But after a few days it's in place, very neatly as ever when our son-in-law completes a project.

We are enthusiastic, Kitty is more guarded. She can't quite see the use of the cat flap. While there was just a hole in the door it was perfectly practical as far as she was concerned. She could run in and out whenever she pleased. But that cat flap is in the way now. It's made of opaque plastic and Kitty sits there trying to look out through it. She doesn't want to walk out that way, it's far better just to wait until someone opens the door. That is what she has always done and she's quite happy to keep doing exactly that. Cats like their routine.

We demonstrate that the gate can be opened; we push her towards it. But as always when trying to force her to do anything, she puts up resistance. It doesn't feel right forcing her through the gap, so we try other methods. We close the door and put her favorite food on the other side. She cannot see it through the cat flap. Maybe she is not hungry enough, at any rate she is willing to wait. Only when we point out that the food is there, while holding the flap open for her, does she trouble herself to come through.

Interfering helpfulness has stifled many good initiatives. The best results are achieved when we leave Kitty in peace and let her take care of it herself. Cats are curious. She walks up to the new opening and feels, with her paw, how it gives way. She crouches a little, pushes with her nose, and when the flap opens, she extends her front paws outside the door and it does not take long for the rest of her body to follow. The flap clatters slightly as her tail glides through. She's out. Entering is a little more elaborate, she has to get the front of her body into the tunnel before she can push the flap open. Yet, soon enough she has also learned to do this, and by the time we go to Africa one week later she is happily aware of her new freedom and constantly running out and in. It's all very good, and during our trip our son-in-law sends us a text message to let us know that Kitty is in excellent condition.

I have always considered it important for doors to be closed. I learned this as a boy. The houses were not as well insulated in those days, and drafts from the door were an abomination. "Close the door!" all the grown-ups used to holler when we children ran out and in and left the doors open behind us. Cats have an entirely different view of it. They hate closed doors and love it when they are left ajar, so they can go wherever they please at any time. When we leave Kitty, we make sure all the doors are left half-open so she can move about inside the house and come and go through her cat flap. We have never seen any evidence that she abuses this freedom.

Maybe in spite of all she finds it quite dull being on her own. Once in early summer we were gone for a whole week, and when we came back late at night Kitty was sitting in the drive by the carport. It looked as if she had been waiting for us, and when my wife got out of the car she immediately came running, headbutting her legs, and purring. It was difficult not to have a bad conscience. That was probably the time we decided to get a cat flap, so that she could at least sleep indoors and eat her food in peace.

Do cats have a notion of time? Does it make any difference to Kitty if we are gone for a week or just a day? Sometimes I think there is a difference, and our daughter is convinced of it. The first time she comes to give food to Kitty, she only seems interested in the chow and nothing else. But a few days later she wants a bit of interaction and feels that someone ought to be playing with her or petting her. At such times she may even want to lie in our daughter's lap, which otherwise she is not much disposed to do.

So I like to think that she misses us. After all, I often think of her when we are away, and it seems more equal if she, in turn, is wondering when we'll be coming back. But it's doubtful. Cats probably do not go around missing one. They live in the present, which does not necessarily preclude her feeling pleased when we turn up after being away for a few days.

Maybe in spite of all Kitty does have a form of social dependence? When we are in the garden she often dogs our heels and when we are upstairs she usually sleeps somewhere nearby: not in our laps, not at our feet, but somewhere close by. And when later we go downstairs to bed it doesn't take long before she comes padding after us. The night is mostly spent in her mistress's bed. In the morning she often comes close to our faces and when she rubs her face against my cheek it almost feels like a kiss.

All this seems very intimate and sweet. But science informs me that cats have scent glands under their chin and forehead, and that Kitty's ceremonious greeting is actually a marking of territory, more or less like when a dog lifts its hind leg against a streetlight. When she seems to be affectionate and fond in the mornings it may just be her way of taking care of her belongings.

Biologists speak of parasites, organisms that live in other animal's nests. Many of these parasites are fairly unwholesome figures: fleas, lice, wall lice, or other bloodsuckers hiding in a birdhouse, a warm pelt, or in people's clothes and homes. It can be a fairly successful strategy, but obviously the hosts do all they can to get rid of these uninvited guests. Others try to ensure a better welcome.

As we know, human beings do not rule the planet, but the social Hymenoptera do: wasps, bees, bumblebees, and, above all, ants. Ants exist in practically every habitat and their successful societies, in which there is always a supply of food, are heaving with unwanted visitors. A small beetle known as *Claviger* lives in anthills, preferably those built by the little yellow meadow ant, common in Sweden. There, *Claviger* feels comfortable, because the little beetle is so well taken care of by its hosts, who tend to its needs in every conceivable way, more or less as we do with Kitty. Things can even go so far that the ants start neglecting their own duties to house and home, in order to devote themselves to their beloved little beetles. Things have not gone so adrift with us, I hope.

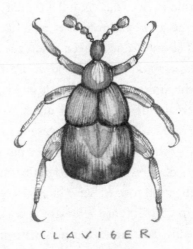

CLAVIGER

So why are beetles so beloved of the ants? Well, because they have large yellow tufts of hair on their hind parts, and from these hairs they produce a glandular secretion that the ants find irresistible. It is almost like a narcotic of a sort. *Claviger* is not unique in this strategy. The short-wings—a family of beetles about a fifth of an inch across—have come up with the same good idea. They spend the wintry half of the year with the true "fire ant" or red ant, but in the summer they move in with the larger wood ants. Just like *Claviger*, they smell lovely and give off a secretion that the ants adore.

The question is, does our cat use a similar strategy? We find her cute and can't resist her gaze. It's pleasurable to stroke her and we feel loved when she coils herself around our legs and purrs. Maybe we are as enchanted by her as the ants are by their beetle guests, which they love to lick and devote quite as much attention to as their own larvae. Whatever the case, Kitty appeals to our senses—otherwise we would never have let her stay.

If Kitty's coat had looked different I may have felt more coldhearted toward her. I have always been more receptive to cats that are yellow or speckled gray, and actually some cats are rather ugly with multicolored spots in more or less inappropriate places. It has probably also been helpful that Kitty is small and lithe. Beauty is seductive. And although she occasionally sharpens her claws on the upholstery, at least she doesn't eat our grandchildren—whereas some ant guests are impudent enough to consume the offspring of their benefactors. Quite the opposite. Our grandchildren are as entranced as we are by our sweet Kitty.

Things have ended up just as I feared. The beloved parasite has tied us down. As soon as we talk of making a journey, the question comes up, "What do we do about Kitty?" I never thought I'd have to show such consideration. But one can't control everything in life, and Kitty has successfully become a part of the family, so I have to gracefully defer to her on this point. With the help of the cat flap it has become a little easier both for her and us. She doesn't have to freeze in the garden shed when we are away, and we aren't burdened with a bad conscience about it.

8

Cats are predators. Their agile bodies are adapted for ambush and springing at their prey. Their claws are specialized at gripping it, their teeth are made to tear it into small pieces, and their intestinal tract to absorb the nourishment of the meat. Kitty likes hunting mice very much. Not for the sake of food—she gets more than enough of that—but because it is so infernally wonderful to hunt.

Before we had a cat we had no idea there were so many mice in our garden. Now, Kitty repeatedly turns up with a mouse in her mouth, which she brings into our bedroom. Most often this happens at night, preferably at about eleven o'clock when it's time for us to go to sleep. It also happens at about four in the morning, and we are less keen on that, because then we definitely want to sleep. But obviously the mice are active at these times, and Kitty, aware of that fact, goes hunting.

Quite often the mouse is in vigorous health, in a panic but fully capable of rushing off across the floor in a desperate attempt to flee the tormentor. This is exactly what Kitty has been waiting for, because this means the cat-and-mouse game can go on. In other words, she carries her mice inside quite carefully and releases them on the floor, where she amuses herself by chasing them. If the mouse sits still for too long she gives it slap with her paw to make it scamper off, thus giving herself the pleasure of catching it another time.

Sometimes the mouse is already dead when Kitty brings it in. She pokes at it with her paw and when it fails to react, looks disappointed: "What's the matter, don't you want to play anymore?"

The best possible scenario for the mouse is if it manages to squeeze itself under a cupboard or behind a bookcase. The cat can't get at it there, so for the moment it's safe. But Kitty is not one to give up. She knows exactly where her mouse is and she's prepared for a long wait—hours, if necessary—until it reappears. Sometimes she places herself on a chair next to the bookshelf the mouse has sneaked behind. She relaxes, makes herself comfortable, and almost seems to go to sleep, but at the slightest scuffling noise from the mouse she's on tenterhooks. Sometimes she goes to the back of the bookcase and tries to stick her paw behind it, as if to confirm to herself that, for the moment at least, the mouse has the upper hand. In which case all she can do is wait. She deflates herself and seems to fall into a slumber.

We are less amused by Kitty's mouse hunts than she is. We want to sleep and have some peace and quiet in the bedroom, and would rather avoid wild chases under our beds or among our shoes. Occasionally we might try to catch the mouse and throw it back into the garden. At such times the poor mouse has two humans and a cat on its heels, and it desperately looks for some cranny in which to hide itself. It is too much to expect of a terrified mouse that it should understand our friendly intentions. It scampers away and we slide out cupboards and beds in our attempt to grab it.

Sometimes the mouse finds a really good "air-raid shelter." Kitty doesn't have a chance. She just sits there looking around in a melancholy manner for her escaped toy, and when we try to flush out the mouse from its hiding place she finds this an utterly splendid idea. In general, I have a feeling that she finds it fairly entertaining when we all join forces in a mouse hunt.

Sometimes I have a fantasy of someone looking in through the window. It must look pretty comical, an elderly couple and a cat running about in a room behind a mouse, which in every way is trying to escape the mayhem.

Quite often we manage to catch the little rodent. We take it by the tail and lob it out of the window, which we then close. Kitty doesn't understand a thing; suddenly her toy has gone. She walks around, looking in places where she last saw her mouse, or where she senses its scent. In the end she sits on her mistress's bed, preens herself for a while as if to calm her nerves, then curls up and goes to sleep. But a few hours later she wants to go out again.

Whenever we attempt to catch the mouse we usually thread a plastic bag over one hand, and then Kitty sometimes realizes that we are about to confiscate her mouse. She doesn't want this, so she takes the mouse in her mouth and rushes out into the garden through the cat flap. Soon she is back again, still with the mouse in her mouth—and the same circus starts again. After a couple of turns like this the poor mouse is usually worse for wear and lies motionless on the floor when dropped by the cat. She tries to liven it up with a couple of jabs of her paw. Then, while she meows in protest, I pick up the mouse with my plastic bag and give it the *coup de grâce*. A forceful blow with a hard flyswatter is usually enough.

As time passes, we have learned not to take Kitty's mouse hunts so seriously, and occasionally we even leave her to her own devices. The other night she came in with a mouse and was rummaging about for a while, but after that everything grew absolutely quiet. Apparently neither the mouse nor the cat was still in the bedroom, and we fell asleep again. But Kitty did not come and lie in our beds as she usually does, and when we came into the hall in the morning the shoes were even more disordered than usual. There had been a mouse hunt here. Kitty had her head pushed as far as it would go into one of my winter boots, and was fishing about inside with her paw. I grew suspicious, picked up the boot, and felt inside. Sure enough, something warm and furry was squirming at the toe-end of the boot. As I took the boot into the garden, Kitty followed, meowing. I shook the boot, the mouse fell out and the hunt was up again. Suddenly the mouse sat up on its hind legs and looked at the cat, which stopped, arched its back, and glared back. There they stood their ground, the predator and her prey, sharply scrutinizing one another.

It looked almost idyllic, not a life-or-death struggle at all. Coming too close, the mouse was startled, and it darted off with the cat in pursuit. This time the mouse managed to hop into a dense hedge, where Kitty had no chance. After a quarter-hour she had given up, and slunk back inside the house.

On one occasion she brought in a mouse in the middle of the day. My wife was sitting upstairs, so Kitty took her prey up the stairs. It was a pesky little thing, and, trying to escape, came careering down the stairs. Kitty came after in hot pursuit, but where had the mouse gone? Kitty looked around in confusion, while I stood at the foot of the stairs, searching for her victim. Everything had gone very fast, and once Kitty loses her prey she is not particularly adept at finding it again. Suddenly I felt something soft clambering on the inside of my pant leg: the mouse! How it had got there I don't know. Although I am not the sort to panic in a situation like this, I don't especially like having mice in my trousers. So my wife brought a plastic bag to catch the mouse, and I stood there with my trousers dropped around my ankles. The mouse made a desperate bid to get away by making a dash for the front door. We opened it and the mouse hurtled out, while Kitty looked more puzzled than anything.

It's not unknown for her to bring in game other than mice. Once when I woke up—my wife was elsewhere—Kitty sat there staring intently at the corner where the ceramic wood-burning stove is. When I investigated more closely, I saw something fairly large and woolly, lying absolutely still at the very back of the fire chamber. Could it be a rat? No, it didn't look quite like a rat, but I was still reluctant to grab the little thing with my hands. Rats can bite, they rarely brush their teeth, and a bite can become horribly infected, so to be on the safe side I extracted it with the fire poker. In fact it was a rabbit kitten skulking in there; perhaps eight inches long, at a stretch. It was an absolutely ordinary gray rabbit kitten, not one of those hybrid cuddly toys with long hair or floppy ears.

I picked it up with one hand. It seemed absolutely unscathed, though absolutely stiff with terror. How and when Kitty had brought it in I did not know. My wife and I had been away for the last twenty-four hours and I had seen no trace of it when I came home in the evening. But I did find tufts of rabbit hair in several places in the house, and suspected that the cat had carried the fluffy little thing inside by the scruff of its neck, more or less as she would also have done with her own kittens if she'd ever had any.

I took the rabbit kitten outside. The cat meowed in protest. When the rabbit felt the fresh air it started wriggling a little, up until then it had sat still in my hand. Gently I put it down on the lawn. It sat there frozen to the spot. Kitty was still inside the house, she probably didn't understand where her rabbit kitten had gone. Was it the hunting urge or maternal instincts that had made her carry it inside? Maybe a combination of the two. When I went into the garden again a few moments later the little rabbit had gone.

This is the first and last time I ever saw a rabbit in our garden, and I wonder where Kitty found it. Not even in the gardens alongside ours is there any evidence of rabbits. Most likely she caught it by the office building on the other side of the street, where I have seen rabbits on a few rare occasions. Whatever the case, she must have struggled with her burden for quite a distance, and now it was gone. The cat was a little disappointed, but I was very pleased. We have a lot of plants in the garden that rabbits would enjoy for their breakfast, but we'd rather they satisfied their appetite elsewhere.

When I complain about Kitty's habits—of course she can hunt for mice, but must she bring them inside?—people seem to feel that I am being ungrateful. The cat is bringing us a present, they say, she wants to show us that she is taking care of her mouse-hunting duties, and earn herself some praise for it. Instead of taking her mice away from her I ought to pat her on the head and say, "There's a good Kitty." But I have another, more prosaic explanation for her behavior: our bedroom is the center of her territory and one brings one's prey back the lair, where one can enjoy it undisturbed.

Yet at times I have wondered about it. Once we closed the bedroom door when we could hear she was in action, to avoid being disturbed by her games. When I got up in the morning the dead mouse had been placed very precisely outside the bedroom door, but the cat was elsewhere. And a couple of times she has put a dead mouse right in front of me, meowing. It almost seems as if she wants to give me a present, but I am still unsure.

Her predatory ways can also be troubling. She is welcome to take mice, they are mainly trouble after all. But in the winters we usually feed the birds. Quite a number of them come: blue tits, great tits, blackbirds, chaffinches, bramblings, robins, wrens, collared doves, and then of course the corvine birds—magpies, jackdaws, rooks, and crows. Sometimes we have had the pleasure of bullfinches and nuthatches, yes, even goldfinches, although they are quite out of the ordinary. On cold, dark winter days on the verge of spring, we have sat at our kitchen table, drinking coffee, eating marzipan buns with whipped cream, and enjoying the avian activity outside the window.

Nowadays we do not feed the birds during winter, which feels a little miserable. We simply don't want to lay on a spread for the cat. A few times she has brought in redstarts, robins, or greenfinches and we'd rather have them in the garden than as bleeding parcels of feathers on the living room carpet. Frozen, hungry little birds make too easy prey for a cat, and since we had the cat flap put in, there's no way of keeping her inside.

So now we sit drinking our morning coffee with a cat on the windowsill and no birds outside. While this may sound quite sweet, we do miss our moments with the birds.

We listen to a discussion of the problem on a natural history program on the radio. The cat, actually one of the most important predators in our country, is especially dominant in residential town and city districts. It takes many birds every year, but, the reporter goes on consolingly, the birds seem to be doing all right anyway. Nonetheless, as I already said, we are not keen on sacrificing the robins and wrens to Kitty.

No, we're not especially fond of Kitty's penchant for hunting. We scold her for it, but it's doubtful whether she pays any great attention to this. A cat is a cat and cats are predatory animals. Now that we have "come down with cat" we can only gracefully accept that she has to occasionally give vent to her predatory instincts. And then there's the whole issue of social relationships. One really has to put up with their bad habits.

9

We often wonder what Kitty went through before she became our cat. I mean, she had a life before she sat on our garden gate that snowy, gray, and cold November morning. We don't even know how long that life was. When we first met her we guessed that she had been a kitten the previous spring, a "summer cat" during the summer months, thrown out into a harsh reality as autumn set in and her initial kittenish cuteness was beginning to wear off. In which case she would have been about six months old when our paths first crossed.

I still believed it could be so. But the vet who performed the operation checked her mouth and felt that she had been born in 2009, not 2010 as we had thought. In which case she would have seen quite a lot before she ran into us. For instance, she must have survived the fairly harsh winter of 2009 to 2010, which was a snowy, difficult cold season in Skåne. Or perhaps she'd had a home before she turned up at ours?

Speaking of which, where had she come from? We live in the middle of a town. While there is certainly a lot of greenbelt around us, it's not real countryside, just private gardens and parks. Kitty is a typical Swedish farm cat of the sort one can easily spot at any farm, and if we had a farm in the vicinity she might well hail from there. But the nearest farm is several kilometers away and to make her way from there she would have had to cross a fairly sterile expanse of residential and industrial areas. It doesn't strike me as particularly likely. On the other hand, cats are curious. What if she had jumped into the back of a truck, only to find herself locked in and being given an unasked-for lift? A journey like that could have been quite long, and, once she entered the town, thoroughly disoriented, she would then have sought out the best place she could find—our garden shed.

Most exciting of all is the thought that she had managed by herself for a long period, but that the cold autumn and early winter forced her to look for shelter in our garden. In which case she would almost have been like a feral cat—we do find that she sometimes behaves like one. But, as I was saying, how did she survive the earlier winter, which was almost as difficult as the one when she came to us? We will probably never know. A cat can't tell its life story.

As a former psychiatrist, I am convinced that the person one used to be early in life is important for who one becomes and how one feels later in life. An untidy childhood makes for an insecure adult, indecisive in his or her relationships to others, whereas someone who has grown up in a loving environment is secure and benevolent toward others. I don't know if such principles can be applied to cats, but I'd like to think that they can. Let me see if this holds water.

Kitty sought us out and was very determined about being our cat. At the same time she was a little anxious. She wasn't pleased about being picked up and she definitely wasn't a cuddly sort looking for immediate body contact. If we suddenly bend down over her she would momentarily seem frightened. The fear of attack from above is deeply imprinted in the brains of all small animals that evolved on the African plains, where there are plenty of hungry eagles. We often perceive her as a fairly shy wildcat, who has only gradually and at her own pace begun to trust that we mean her no harm.

On the other hand, we were hardly accessible from the very start either. Kitty was left to sleep outside through the icy winter nights. Maybe it was not so strange that she wondered where she stood with us. Were we dismissive or loving? If Kitty had been clearer about wanting close contact with us, we would very likely have softened much quicker. She was definitely aware that humans could be a resource; otherwise she would hardly have approached us. At quite an early stage we also had the feeling that she knew goodies could be kept in a refrigerator. She also seemed familiar with the TV. We don't watch the TV very much, but whenever we do, Kitty likes to stay fairly close. It's as if she associates the whole situation with security; from time to time she looks at the screen, but usually not. The atmosphere is cozy and the humans sit still, apart from clattering with a coffee cup or a glass. The first few times Kitty sought out her mistress's lap was when she was sitting in front of the TV.

At some point in the early stages of our acquaintance with Kitty, our grandchild had a temperature. Unable to go to school, he spent the day on our sofa, watching TV. Kitty lay at his side the whole time, which was how they became best friends. It was warm and nice for both of them, and the cat seemed to appreciate the soft murmuring of the children's programs in the background. Kitty likes children and she was acting the part of the perfect family cat. Was that what she had been before?

It would be difficult to find a more housebroken animal that Kitty. Both food and drink are taken in at the front, and it seems feasible that something must come out of the back end. Yet as a rule neither of us ever see her peeing or pooing. She manages these matters very discreetly, as is customary in all cats. One of the few exceptions was that week when we had to keep her in the house after the operation, so that the wound on her stomach would have time to heal. That was when we bought a litter tray, poured litter into it, and put it by the kitchen door. Kitty did not hesitate for a moment about using this facility for her convenience. Had she been a house cat for a part of her life and learned what a cat tray was?

No, I don't think one can draw any such conclusions. It is probably rather the case that litter trays appeal to the innate instincts of cats. When relieving oneself, one first rakes the ground a little, does what needs to be done, and then rakes over the evidence. It would not be possible to do all of this anywhere in our house except in the litter tray, and we have only ever had a litter tray for that one week. In fact she did once start scraping the soil of the pot holding our two-yard-high coffee tree. But when she tried to squat on the edge of the pot we interrupted her.

———

I like speculating like this on Kitty's past. I reflect on her habits and wonder how she has learned them. I psychologize and interpret her relationship to adults, children, and dogs: as I have said she likes children but has no regard at all for dogs. In the end, how far can one psychologize a cat—and yet, how is it possible not to? I will address one question at a time.

Is not a cat's behavior fairly preprogrammed, a series of reactions that natural selection in all its wisdom has engendered in a little predator that creeps about in low African bush vegetation? This is not a far-reaching psychological interpretation. A cat's behavior is just as determined by its inherited nature as by the fact that it has two triangular ears that can be turned in different directions, two sharp eyes that can find its prey even in the pitch-black tropical night, and a nose with a sense of smell that may not be as sensitive as a dog's, but is considerably more acute than the fairly blunt olfactory sense of humans. Whenever the personalities of two cats are subtly different it is mainly because of their hereditary disposition. Freud should stay out of this. It may sound objective and unsentimental, maybe even scientific. But is it true?

Our son believes so. When Kitty dislikes his dogs it is because all cats dislike dogs, and not because Kitty has any particularly traumatic experiences of dogs. Maybe he is right, but in spite of all I would like to believe that what she went through before she met us is not insignificant in its effect on her personality.

It's not that I believe the inner lives of cats can get quite as dizzy as humans manage to make theirs. Cats are just too "dumb" for that. But surely it's feasible that they draw certain conclusions from their experiences. Even if a kitten's life is considerably less complicated than a child's, both human infants and kittens are mammals, and all young mammals need protection and a certain amount of care at the beginning. Otherwise they do not survive, neither in a physical nor mental sense. In short, I believe that even with cats, if they are secure it could have something to do with their early experiences. Sometimes I find that our cat seems unsure about her position in relation to humans, which makes me wonder what she has been through in her life. But of course I will never know.

I am psychologizing again. It's as if I can't stop myself. And, of course, as a former psychiatrist it has been my job to engage with people's thoughts and feelings. Anyway, our entire age is about psychologizing. Never before have people been so interested in talking about themselves and never before have others been so prepared to listen to them. And yet these cultural circumstances are not enough on their own to explain why I am immersing myself in the inner life of my cat. It seems that psychologizing is also deeply rooted in the biological nature of humans.

Most primates are social, and humans are the most social of them all. Our thought processes evolved in a flock, where it was important to keep track of what others might want. A good starting point when one wishes to understand others, can be to assume that they think and feel more or less as oneself, and that as a consequence they have plans and intentions underlying what they do. As humans, we do not only apply this kind of analysis to other humans, but also—for example—to cats. Sometimes we even have a notion that dead machines such as computers and cars have an inner soul, and we take out our irritation on them when they don't do what we tell them to do.

Certainly Kitty's actions sometimes reveal her intentions, and she quite often trusts in our ability to read these intentions. She walks toward the closed door and looks first at the doorknob and then at me. Being her obedient servant, I put away my newspaper, rise from my comfortable armchair, and go to the door to open it for her. She immediately walks out of the door and I do not get so much as a glance of thanks. Of course she sometimes senses what I am about to do. When I get up in the morning she knows it's a good time to purr and slink around my legs, because this fairly often leads to my going to the kitchen and giving her food. But in spite of all this, I do think that the intentions she ascribes to us are very few compared to those we ascribe to her. And she really knows how to exploit to the full that we are always thinking about what she may be wanting from us. It's an aspect of her skill as a domestic animal.

Kitty is subjected to our irresistible drive to read intentions and feelings into the creatures we encounter in our day-to-day lives. Probably we read much too much into situations, often sensing things that are not there at all. Whenever we do not do what she wants us to do, we feel that Kitty gives us a reproachful look. But can a cat really feel reproachful? To ask, and even beg, are skills it excels at—but can it feel reproachful? When we imagine that she is disappointed in us and we feel guilty about it, we are probably ascribing feelings to her that she does not even have.

The other day I accidentally trod on Kitty's tail. Thank goodness she was not hurt, but it was painful. I had gone down to the kitchen and she had followed without my noticing—cats move quickly and soundlessly. I didn't have a clue where she was, and when I stepped back I felt something soft under my slipper and heard a loud meowing. I lifted my foot at once and Kitty darted off, sat in a corner and gave me a reproachful look—at least that was how it seemed to me. I felt bad about it. I really do not want to hurt Kitty, quite the opposite, all I want is for her to trust in me.

But how does one apologize to a cat? My spontaneous reaction was to take her in my arms, give her a hug, and make assuaging little gestures. A human would understand this, a dog would probably also understand it. But Kitty? She is not very fond of being picked up as it is, but when I press my cheek to her little face she purrs in spite of all, which makes me feel good. Yet fundamentally she is totally unconcerned with my need to be forgiven by her. That tail episode was not such a big thing, now she wants the chow that she was after, and she stays with me in the kitchen.

I am just hoping that she won't bear a grudge. Some dogs do, but I have never noticed such tendencies in Kitty. Cats are probably too asocial to bear a long-term grudge to other creatures. Darwin suggests that a dog can feel the difference between someone unintentionally stumbling over them, or kicking them on purpose. He may well be right, but I am not as sure that a cat can make a similar distinction. If cats think at all, they do not think socially.

Can one understand animals by using one's capacity for empathy? The question has been discussed with great seriousness using rigorous scientific parameters. In the mid-1900s, the humanizing of animals—anthropomorphism—was a breach of procedure that no scientist could properly adopt, if he or she wanted to be taken seriously. Anyone who wished to be scientific, had to scrupulously observe the impressions, the stimuli, to which an animal was being subjected, then dispassionately register its reactions and behaviors. Everything that existed between what the animal—or, as a matter of fact, the human—experienced, and how it behaved as a consequence, was forever encased in a "black box." To try to enter into how an animal thought and felt was considered nothing but naïve sentimentality.

Nowadays, we have a slightly less condemning attitude to this deadly sin. Not least, researchers looking into the social life of our closest relatives, the great apes, often believe that the emotional life of apes is rather like our own. The groundbreaking thinker here was Jane Goodall, a young British secretary who lived with a group of chimpanzees in Tanzania. She was passionately curious and minutely scrupulous in her documentation, but sufficiently unschooled not to bother with scientific purism. Without reflecting very much about it, she gave names to the subjects of her study, and felt that their thoughts and emotions were similar to her own. Her approach proved very successful. Scientists simply understood these animals better once they assumed that they had more or less comparable re-actions to our own.

Could it not be the same thing with cats? If I assume that Kitty's inner life is much like my own, do I not then have a better position from which to understand her than if I merely see her as a guest from another planet? Yes, I'd like to think so.

But perhaps I am letting my daydreams run away with me. I so desperately want to understand Kitty and grasp how she has become the personality that I see. I work my way into her skull and interpret, interpret, interpret. . . . But a cat is a cat and cats are quite unlike us humans. It's quite another thing with Jane Goodall's chimpanzees. They are "our cousins," after all.

Of course I get it all wrong when I interpret Kitty's intentions. But does it really matter? Is not the whole idea of having household pets precisely that we *do* humanize them? When I am close to breakdown about my Internet connection not "wanting to" work, Kitty comes into my study and rubs herself against my legs. When I pick her up, she purrs. It feels as if she wants to console me. Fundamentally I can understand that her intentions are probably quite different, but it makes me feel good to imagine her as empathetic. So I pet her a little more and she keeps purring.

Humans caress each other with language. Young lovers talk incessantly. They gauge every signal from their partner and their words weave themselves into a sort of fabric of confirmation. What is actually said may not greatly matter. But when conflict arises, silences grow icy and the few words that are spoken are rather like sword blades, shredding the togetherness rather than rebuilding it.

We are fond of our Kitty and we are always talking to her. Our tone of voice is caressing and musical, almost like when talking to a baby: "Little darling," we say. I don't think the cat understands what we are saying. Can she even interpret our caressing tone? Whatever the case, we can't stop ourselves from talking to her. We are humans and these soft words are our way of showing the cat that we care about her.

Is our Kitty at all interested in the fellowship with her that we spend so much time building? Or does she only want food and a roof over her head—tasty food without any effort on her part, soft armchairs and beds where she can curl up and sleep? She helps herself to all these benefits, takes them all for granted, in a way that feels both unreflected upon and forthright. There is no doubt that she is satisfied. But does she feel grateful?

Doris Lessing has written a little book, more than anything a long essay, on her cat Rufus—his name given him on account of his red coat. Rufus is disheveled when he becomes a part of Lessing's household, where there are already two other well-fed cats. His coat is unkempt, his ribs are visible, and he drinks water so copiously that Lessing immediately suspects he is having a problem with his kidneys, an assumption that is confirmed by the vet. The cat-loving author obviously assumes responsibility for this miserable creature. Rufus is given food, he is permitted to sleep indoors, and in the meantime he is taken several times to see the vet. Slowly and methodically he fights for his place in the lap of the Nobel Prize–winning author. The other smug household cats have to make some room and come to terms with the fact that their position as favorites is no longer quite as self-evident.

Much of the book's charm lies in Lessing's descriptions of the personalities of the cats. One of her old, well-established household cats is playful and curious—and has a scientific nature, Lessing suggests. The other is a big, beautiful, and self-satisfied salon cat convinced of its own irresistible pull on others, and therefore always entitled to the top spot in its mistress's affections. Rufus is an outsider, a sinuous and determined proletarian who after a hard life is now supremely thankful to have found a good home at last, and be able to enjoy his mistress's attentions. But he remains stubbornly conscious of the need to edge out her earlier favorites.

There is no doubt in my mind about cats having different personalities. But can a cat really feel grateful? Is not Lessing's conviction that Rufus feels indebted to her a way of creating emotional ties that might not actually be there? I suspect her of humanizing her cats because she can't stop herself. She would be thankful if she were in Rufus's position, and like other humans she spontaneously and unreflectively imagines that all the creatures she meets have feelings and thoughts much like her own.

Sometimes I wonder if the inner life of cats emanates from their tails. What else would they have their tails for? It certainly looks elegant when they sit and curl their tails around themselves, and rather haughty when Kitty comes trotting down the stairs, her tail aloft, its uppermost quarter-length coquettishly waving.

Are cats expressing something with their tails? Or are tails just a ballast that they have to bear as a reminder of their status as vertebrate animals: a head at the front, two extremities somewhere in the middle and then an appendage at the back end, more or less the basic plan for their kind. Few have done anything really useful with their tails, spider monkeys being the glaring exception. Many vertebrate animals have gone the other way and simply got rid of this appendage that mainly seemed to impede them: frogs, ourselves, and some other apes. And then of course there are some close relatives of the cats, the lynxes, who only have a stump at the back but seem to do very well without anything more.

So why do cats have a tail? Is it to express feelings? If so, to whom? Humans tell each other a great deal using mime and body posture. If we had tails I am sure we would have thousands of ways of using them. Tail presentation would be an important signifier of class; amorous couples would intertwine their tails. A bow on the tail would tell a thousand words, or why not decorate it with flowers? Fashion designers would come up with an infinite variety of imaginative creations. Maybe one could dye one's tail or have the fur trimmed in various patterns. Actors would be forced to rehearse gestures of the tail and it would all be marvelously effective. Just imagine how much one could say with a tail! When approaching the idea imaginatively like this, it almost saddens me not to have one. I am assuming of course that our tails would be furry and covered in a pelt, as with cats or monkeys. If they were bald or curly like pigtails it would mostly be disgusting.

But what is the purpose of Kitty's tail? T. S. Eliot's

"curious cats" may move in London's club circles or show up at the theater, but most other cats don't follow their example. They stroll about on their own in the terrain, looking for small rodents or nestlings and for this they have no need of a tail—in fact a tail can even get in the way. So what's the use of it?

When Kitty lies there licking the tip of her tail, holding onto it with all four paws, we find her very endearing. Often she prolongs her grooming much more than she needs to do from a hygiene perspective, and we make the association of a child sucking its thumb. We can appreciate Kitty's tail, and we find that it contributes to her beauty. But while we may perceive that she is waving her tail with a sort of pride, or trailing it in a sort of melancholy manner, we can't be sure whether we are interpreting her correctly. The reason for cats having tails remains one of their deepest secrets. I am not even sure whether science has an answer for it.

Where am I really trying to get to with all these speculations about Kitty's inner life? All I know for certain is that we will never really understand one another. I will never become another Doctor Dolittle who can talk to the animals, and she will not turn into Findus nattering away and correcting Pettson's misjudgments.

Despite this, we seem to get through to each other and we have a lovely time together. I do suspect that our relationship is based on a good deal of misunderstanding. So what! Long live misunderstanding, as long as it does us a power of good.

10

Apparently the French avant-garde poet Jean Cocteau once said that he preferred cats to dogs for the plain reason that there was no such thing as a police cat. The willingness of dogs to loyally defer to humans, he declared, was a veritable catastrophe.

For dogs, a sense of belonging is more important than freedom. In this respect they are very much like many humans. Rather than being alone, they accept the lowest position in the hierarchy. The dog is submissive to its master and mistress, and is willing to enter into military service when ordered to attack. In short, dogs are the perfect servants or cohorts of the police. In a worst-case scenario they can develop Fuhrer traits. He who occupies the bottom rungs of the ladder is often keen to exert what little power he has, for instance, by barking.

Little cat, little cat
walking so alone
tell me whose cat are you—
I'm damned well my own.

This is the "Stockholm rhyme," a translation of one of Piet Heins's famous "Grook" aphorisms—he was a Danish furniture designer, poet, and much else—and it is not coincidental that it was composed during the German occupation. Cats, unlike dogs, are the perfect symbol of autonomy.

Kitty embodies this idea, she chooses her own path. When we call for her she comes if it suits her but not by a long shot every time, and if we pat the sofa or our knees she does not pay the slightest attention to our exhortations for her to come and lie in these places, unless they coincide with her own wishes. Fundamentally I am quite satisfied about this.

Probably I am a "cat person." I have always had difficulties identifying with any particular group. While I was in medical practice I liked to feel that I was working *alongside* my colleagues and taking take care of more or less the same tasks, but not really associated with them. It was also like this while I worked with biologists or theology researchers. I moved freely among them, was appreciated by them and felt perfectly content in their company, but always opted to stay a little on the outside. I wanted to be among them but not, properly speaking, one *of* them. One could call this a sense of autonomy, social incompetence, or maybe, more judiciously, arrogance. Or, I believe, it could even be cowardice, a fear of throwing oneself wholeheartedly into a task one is prepared to take seriously.

Kitty is also an outsider. She has chosen to live with us, but she doesn't imagine for a moment that she is a part of our flock. Dogs, I often think, are out of their minds; they can't even distinguish between animals and humans. Our little Kitty does not make mistakes of that kind. She knows that we are we, while she is, "damned well my own." I can't deny that I am compelled by this asocial—please note I did not say "antisocial"—trait in her. It doesn't mean she can't be friendly. She can purr and be sweet and cuddly, in just the same way as I'm capable of being sociable and entertaining. But at heart both Kitty and I want to walk our own roads. In that respect we are the same.

Kitty's independence gives her and us certain freedoms, because she doesn't have to hang on our heels. But it also creates a sense of insecurity for us all. She is left to her own devices and we do not always know where she is. "Where is Kitty?" we ask ourselves several times every day, and the answer is often, "I don't have a clue!" One only feels calm when she's lying asleep in her basket by my workstation or on my wife's bed, but I still want it to be her choice to be lying there, and I want her to be able to leave at any moment.

But sometimes I find Kitty almost too independent. She likes to lie down in places where it is difficult to see her, and when I want to be with her, or stroke her, she sometimes reacts with irritation and moves off. Then I feel rejected. After all, we keep her fed and housed, surely she could make a bit of an effort to be available?

People say that the cat is the only household pet that has chosen to be a pet. This may be true if one ignores the dog, eternal companion of the human species, having already been there when the first representatives of our kind were wandering the savannas of Africa. While horses, sheep, and cattle, and, yes, even elephants, were caught and domesticated, the cats sought out human habitation entirely on their own initiative. And it wasn't even the humans they were interested in.

For as long as our ancestors were still living by hunting and gathering nuts and roots, the cats were not the least bit interested in them. The savanna teemed with mice and rats, in the summers there was a host of bird eggs hatching, and sometimes there were great swarms of locusts. The agile hunters suffered no deprivation. But when humans started cultivating and harvesting some ten thousand years ago, they became a focus of interest for the cats. The many small rodents, which cats were so skilled at hunting, tended to gather in the granaries: the rat on the seed and the cat on the rat.

Genetic research has tracked all house cats, whether of pampered or unpampered varieties, to the Middle East and Egypt, and this certainly seems credible. These were the areas where arable farming first took hold, and the wildcats were not slow in helping themselves to the new possibilities created by agriculture.

I have actually seen an African wildcat. It lay curled up in the chilly winter's night a several miles outside Satara, the big tourist camp in the Kruger National Park in

South Africa. The spot is well known for its healthy
population of lions and leopards, and these big cats
are also comparatively easy to see on the open savanna. A true wildcat is significantly more difficult to
find. It's nocturnal and shy and its mixed shades of
gray merge perfectly into the dry bush vegetation.

We had bought tickets for a night safari. A short
while after we had rolled out into the monotonous landscape, one of the tourists called out, something had been
spotted in the darkness. When the spotlights of the
safari vehicle illuminated the little cat it squinted with
its eyes but stayed still on the ground and allowed
itself to be perused. The wildcat's face was strikingly
similar to our Kitty's, and it kept its tail neatly coiled
around its body, as cats have a custom of doing. Its
coat was more evenly gray and lighter than Kitty's,
but the dark bands between its ears, so clearly visible
on Kitty, were quite evident on the wild version. No
one could doubt that our house cat at home in the bed
and the wildcat out on the deserted African savanna
were one and the same species. But the cat in the
neighboring block, which is white with large gray
patches between its back and head, is less like a wildcat
than ours.

While Pekinese dogs, Icelandic horses, and brindled
red Swedish cows are all products of human intervention, the boundaries between a wildcat and a domesti-

cated cat have never been quite as clear. Most cats that live in the immediate vicinity to humans have kept much of the appearance and characteristics of a wildcat. Even the most high-bred long-haired cat or Siamese retains more of its wild nature than the most basic mongrel dog.

While dogs soon integrated with the human flock, the connection between cats and humans had a quite different dynamic. The task of humans, from the cat perspective, was to amass resources, which in turn attracted what mattered to the cats, namely voles and mice. The cats retained their personal integrity.

Cats never became the hunting partners of humans, as the dogs did, nor did they become working slaves like the oxen and the horses; they did not deliver milk or meat like the cows, sheep, or pigs. But humans did soon notice that it was practical to have a kitty cat in the granary. They were left with more grain for themselves and there were fewer rat droppings in what remained. The cute kittens with their large, pleading eyes and their soft fur soon became firm favorites with the children—almost like living soft toys. The cats were tolerated and even appreciated. Yet they never quite became the children of the outhouse, as the dogs did, but had to keep to the outer edges of the farm, on the boundary between domesticated and wild animals.

When faithless cats were compared with trusty dogs, the cats always came off worse. "There is a natural antipathy," zoologist Carl von Linné explained to his students, "between cats and people, which no one has been able to distinguish or explain." And one thing was certain: whoever kept a cat in the bed fell prey to sickness. Linné loved animals. He wrote tenderly and with insight about his guenon monkey and Sjupp, his raccoon, both of which lived with him at his house in Uppsala. Where did he get that loony idea that it was mortally dangerous to sleep with a cat in the bed? Did the unwillingness of cats to behave in an ingratiating manner—both Diana, the monkey, and Sjupp were very sociable—turn him into a skeptic when it came to these dainty, clean animals, which present absolutely no danger to humans?

Nor did Sven Nilsson, professor of zoology at Lund University in the mid-1800s, have a lot of good to say about cats. A dog was trustworthy, a cat wasn't. Dogs were loyal hunting partners, cats competed with them for small game. Certainly they were good enough at keeping rats and mice at bay, but apart from that they were also seen as vermin. The European wildcat, Sven Nilsson claimed, was "a dangerous predator" that caught both birds and fish, and tame house cats had retained much of their wild relative's character. It would never be possible to "entirely eradicate" their "devious, malicious disposition." He provided telling examples: a tame cat that had gone feral in Västra Odarslöv several miles outside Lund had killed several lambs and there were even cases of cats having "murdered small, defenseless toddlers in the cradle" or "severely injured elderly individuals." Keeping a cat in the bedroom was absolutely inappropriate. When a cat saw the pulsating carotid vein on the throat it was stimulated to attack: it shredded the blood vein by clawing or biting, and as a consequence the cat owner ran the risk of dying of blood loss. Cats, wrote Sven Nilsson, are bloodthirsty and cruel, they attack "defenseless animals" even when they are not hungry and have no need to do so. At the same time they are lazy and cowardly.

It's hardly a flattering description, but in Sven Nilsson's time it was quite in order to be moralistic about animal behavior. And after all there is some substance in what he is saying. Kitty does take mice and birds just because she finds it enjoyable. As Sven Nilsson points out she is quite lazy, and certainly she may seem a bit of a coward. "Better run than be sorry!" seems to be her maxim, but I find it difficult to get especially upset about this. Nowadays we tend not to moralize about animals. The zeitgeist has changed.

Linné and Nilsson perceived cats as false and undependable. Yet dogs, always alert to their master's command and ready to obey his every wish, were seen as "Man's best friend." Loyalty—not freedom—was the ideal. By the early 1900s, intellectual snobs had other ideas, and Jean Cocteau regarded cats as suitably rebellious symbols of the indifference to social status that was regarded as desirable in the literary and artistic coteries that he made his own. In these circles, freedom and independence were more important than unimpeachable loyalty.

Maybe it is no coincidence that it has become increasingly popular to keep cats as pets. Modern people like to see themselves as free of ties and duties, not as creatures of the herd. It comes easily to them to identify with cats. The almost demonstrative reluctance of cats to own up to their dependence on their masters and mistresses seems more attractive to us than the neurotic desire of dogs to please us. Who would not prefer to be more wild than tame?

Our cat chose us, we did not choose her. That is what cats have done for thousands of years and that must be why they hold up their tails so proudly. They are autonomous individualists, who refuse to find their place in the order of precedence—just as independent as many people dream they could also be.

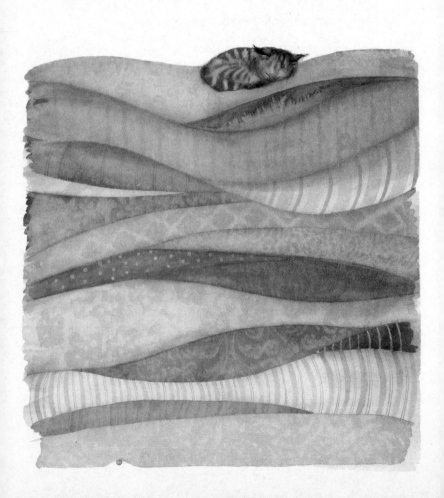

11

Whatever qualities one can learn from a cat, diligence is not one of them. In the way of all predators, it rarely devotes any energy to what does not create immediate results, either in terms of food or the possibility of mating. A sleeping cat is one of the most peaceful sights one can see.

Nature may seem splendid and wasteful, but fundamentally it is niggardly. Natural selection is a hard taskmaster. All tendencies that do not contribute to their own dispersal are mercilessly isolated and discarded. An organism must have food in order to live on, and a little bit of finery can sometimes be needed to awaken the "ladies'" interest. But any unnecessary frippery—whether in behavior or appearance—is cleared away. The noteworthy point is not why a cat chooses to sleep a large part of its life away; the actual question is why humans don't do the same?

People today hardly give themselves time to sleep. Instead we are constantly busy doing a whole lot of things that might be considered entirely useless. We have to read that book, make that telephone call, or finish that job. We have to have a gossip with our friends, relatives, or colleagues about the latest, or keep ourselves informed of what's going on in the community, at the workplace, or in the political sphere. We devote time and money to dressing ourselves effectively, eating the right food, and keeping track of the latest fashion trends . . . really, is there anything we are unwilling to waste our time on? Cats don't have to deal with all these problems, or should we call them topics of amusement?

When I relax it is often an integral part of a greater plan: "I'll take the chance to relax now, because in an hour I have to . . ." A cat doesn't bother with these kinds of provisory factors, it lives fully in the present. When Kitty curls up in her basket it's as if she could never be anything but relaxed.

Linné took a similar line. Cats, he said, are the most comfortable of all animals, they "can lie by the stove all day without any concern for keeping themselves fed, or the cares of tomorrow." Maybe the restlessly active Linné, always anxiously guarding over his own status, envied the cats their untroubled outlook? I can understand him.

But even if Kitty can't teach me how to get enthused about my work, she may be able to contribute in another sense. When I see her lying curled up in her basket, her muscles in an absolute state of relaxation, she sucks me into her sense of calm. Relaxation is contagious, just like yawning and laughing; her absolute presence in a restful "here and now" also helps me find some rest.

Linné did not only note that cats were extremely comfortable in their nature, he also pointed out that they "sleep readily." A sleeping cat can very quickly transform itself into a very awake cat, with its senses fully engaged and its muscles perfectly prepared for fight or flight. Everything is about very quickly getting a grasp on the present. What happened?—Oh, apparently nothing to worry about! Okay, I'll just curl up again, then. The electric switch in the brain is turned off and once again the cat is totally relaxed.

Among psychotherapists it has become fashionable to talk about "mindfulness"—a healing sense of consciousness in the moment. Cats are the supreme practitioners of this immediate existence, this sense of "now." For instance, there is something prepossessing about cats when they are preening themselves. Slowly and methodically they work their way from back paws, front paws, stomach, and back, with the tail often getting a bit of extra attention. And then, usually, it's time for a bit of rubbing of the face with the front paw, first one and then the other. Kitty seems to feel good while she's engaged in this ritual, this self-absorbed submersion into the joys of grooming, almost like a teenage girl applying her makeup.

Personally I have a great need to concentrate on one thing at a time. Everything unrelated to what I am doing in the moment is irritating to me. For instance, I can't listen to music in the background while I am reading. No, either I read or I listen to music. Both one and the other lay claim to my full attention and I try, with varying degrees of success, to push away everything that is irrelevant. In this respect Kitty is infinitely superior to me.

I love classical music, especially if composed in the last hundred and fifty years. It could be chamber music or string quartets, but also noisy orchestral music such as Tchaikovsky, Mahler, Sibelius, Prokofiev, or Shostakovich, mighty symphonies where orchestras a hundred musicians strong are all pushing their instruments to the utmost. To satisfy my longing for music I have got myself a first-class high-fidelity system with a powerful amplifier and substantial speakers. Kitty probably has no particular interest in music, because whenever I am listening to it she prefers to lie down in another room. But sometimes she goes and lies down on a rug between four-and-a-half-foot-tall loudspeakers. Mahler or Shostakovich may be letting rip, but in the middle of all that noise the cat lies, totally at peace, possibly preening itself a little, before curling up and going to sleep as calmly as if the room had been dead silent.

For a moment I forget the music and watch Kitty in amazement. How can she be so absolutely unaffected? Her hearing is exceedingly acute. She can hear a mouse carefully rustling in the next room, but Mahler literally walloping along with kettledrums and trumpets does not concern her at all, she just calmly continues preening herself. Yet if she hears the key being turned in a lock downstairs, she reacts. As if her triangular ears can filter out all the thunderous noise in order to hear the fine movements of a bird among dry leaves or the sound of a key in a lock. This ability to ignore the irrelevant alarum, in order to be able to immediately register the

unobtrusive but significant sound, is something that I
deeply envy. My own slow, aging-man's senses function
in quite the opposite way: the noise of the street drowns
out the birdsong, the fumes of cars push out the fra-
grance of flowers.

Cats are not only able to distinguish important matters from trivialities, they also have a sense of quality.
On some occasion we yielded and bought a small can
of delicatessen cat food, salmon mousse, as a change
from the usual dry pellets. It was appreciated greatly,
and in time there have been many more such cans
on offer.

But at some point we thought to ourselves that maybe
she could try another, somewhat more modest canned
cat food. And certainly she did sniff at it in a tentative
manner, tasted it cautiously, licked at the sauce or jelly,
before going back to the dry pellets, which she's accustomed to and likes reasonably well. The remains of the
tinned food are left on the dish, where, over time, they
begin to look unappetizing. Her whole attitude is like
the refined position of the gourmet, presented with
dishes of either greater or lesser appeal. It's as if Kitty
would say, "Why eat chopped pork and drink beer, when
there are oysters and champagne?" She simply ignores
the basic canned food, but when we defer to her and

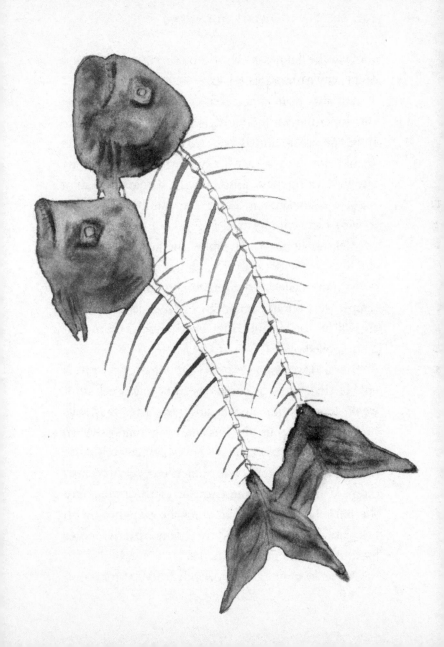

get out the luxury food, she purrs with satisfaction and eats with notable relish.

As far as we're concerned it's a matter of principle: the supermarket food only costs marginally more than the other canned food, but the way we see it she should not always have to have the best. We don't always have the best, after all. The whole pleasure of luxury, we imagine, is that it is maximized by varying it with the ordinary in-between. But Kitty couldn't care less about moral principles, she just eats the food she likes. If she doesn't get it, then—fine—she'll make do with dry pellets if she gets too hungry, which won't happen very often. Sooner or later, she seems to think, there'll be something better on the table. Our cat is quite spoiled.

She also wants variety. While dogs cooperatively gobble the same old chow day after day, week after week, month after month, and year after year, cats have ideas. With us, she has eaten tuna mousse with great pleasure every time we have had reason to give her something special, but suddenly it won't do anymore. When we get the can out of the refrigerator she purrs just as usual, but when the contents are on her plate she has a sniff and then demonstratively goes back to crunching her dry pellets.

Our sense of morality is offended: "What rubbish is

this! There's nothing wrong with this food, so you had better eat it up before you get anything else." The tuna mousse is left where it is and nothing else is offered. When near evening she still hasn't eaten it, we put it back in the tin and put it in the refrigerator. The next morning it is brought out again and once more it is met by disdainful looks and a lot of eager munching of dry pellets: Don't get the idea that I'm not hungry, but I'm tired of this—and I'd rather leave it.

I'm one of those people who tries to live up to certain principles but constantly fails in my attempts. A third time the tuna mousse was brought out and met with the same disdain. And now I don't have the energy to hold on to my principles any longer: "So let's try the salmon mousse, then." And yes, thank goodness it seems to be good enough. A tin costs about seventy-five cents so it doesn't seem worth making a big fuss about it. The problem is, it feels like a moral failing on my side, I should have a bit more control of how we do things. But as for the blessed cat, she seems pleased more than anything. She is totally indifferent to moral principles.

Kitty's philosophy of pleasure is not only limited to food. For instance, certain places are more comfortable to sleep in than others. As I have said, she usually spends most of the night on a towel on her mistress's bed. But when we bought new, fresh duvet covers she soon realized that it was more appealing to lie on them, rather than on the towel with its rougher fabric. She placed herself very precisely next to the towel. The message was clear.

By now I suppose the reader has long since realized that my cat is an utter hedonist without any scruples—a creature of pleasure without any sense of shame about it, who simply helps herself quite shamelessly to the best of what is on offer. I feel there is something attractive about this. In her short life, Kitty has been through a good deal. She has been homeless in the winter nights and she has been a spoiled lounge cat. And her strength throughout has been her ability to make the best of the situation. Of course in a pinch one *can* sleep in a basket among hard gardening implements, if the alternative is to lie unsheltered in the open in a freezing-cold winter's night. But clearly a soft bed with a towel is better, not to mention a bed with brand-new satin sheets.

I can respect this sort of approach to life. Kitty does not hesitate to choose what is better whenever possible, but on the other hand she has also had to put up with fairly miserable conditions when nothing better

was offered. Kitty won't teach me how to be industri-
ous, but she does have a certain amount of patience in
the face of various sore trials. And I can certainly do
with some of that.

12

Spring has come again. Snowdrops and winter aconites have long since flowered, and even the crocuses are starting to look a little tired. This is Lund's blue period, the gardens of the so-called professorial quarter are covered in scilla. In a few weeks it's time for the magnolia. The buds of the early blooming variety in our garden have already started swelling, but the flower that is supposed to be in bloom by the time the student choirs welcome spring, is biding its time.

It's our second spring "with cat." And Kitty is very pleased that the winter is over. She is outside a great deal in the daytime and appreciates that we are, too. But she is also good at keeping herself occupied with the hunting of butterflies and bumblebees. She brings in the odd mouse.

It is now almost a year and a half since Kitty sat on

the garden gate, begging us to let her in. Since then, she has established a solid position in our everyday lives, and I am happy about that for the most part. As long as it does not involve anything worse than finding oneself "with cat," it is probably good for one's development to be exposed to something unexpected. Elderly people have a tendency to become fixed about certain habits. Kitty has forced us to trial a few new ones, and this has been mainly beneficial.

But cats are also creatures of routine. They do certain things at certain times of the day, almost ritually. Kitty sleeps in her mistress's bed, but wakes at some point in the small hours and goes outside through her cat flap. What she gets up to out there we don't have a notion of, except when she comes in with a mouse, and this—thank goodness—doesn't happen so very often. When it's time for us to get up at about half past six in the morning, she is quickly in position, rubbing herself against our legs and purring. She wants to say hello and have some breakfast, in fact plenty of it. At this time of the morning she is hungry, later in the day she may appreciate the odd morsel but nowhere near as much as in the morning.

Then she goes outside for another stroll, probably to take care of her bodily needs, but quite quickly she is back inside the house. In the dark and cold time of year, she likes to seek out a window with a radiator beneath. There she can sit for quite some time, looking out in a very relaxed manner, almost like a person deep in thought in front of a beautiful landscape. After that, it's very common for her to make her way to the basket in my study, there to preen herself for a few moments before curling up and going to sleep.

But if we get busy with something in the kitchen or our grandchildren visit us, she wakes up and is quickly on the scene to investigate whether something exciting is going on or any food can be had. If we leave her on her own to run some errands or take a walk, she usually reacts as soon as she hears the key in the lock. Often she is standing right inside the door even before we've had time to unlock it. If the weather is pleasant she will go out for most of the afternoon, but if it's nasty she's more comfortable in her basket. As evening approaches she'll go out for a walk, generally staying out until after we have gone to bed, but usually around midnight she is back in my wife's bed. The day is over.

Of course these routines do change if something out of the ordinary happens, but in principle her rhythm is quite similar from day to day, which suits me just fine. Like most writers I know, I keep to certain routines. If one does not have a manager or any fixed working hours, one has to impose some of one's own structure on the working day. Walking around, waiting for inspiration, is hardly ever worthwhile. People say appetite comes through eating, and for me at least, inspiration—if it comes at all—tends to arrive while I am at work. So if I don't have something else that needs doing, I sit down at the computer directly after breakfast and try to stay there until lunchtime; I go back for a shorter amount of time in the afternoon. In other words my best working hours coincide with the times Kitty likes to lie in her basket. We share some companionship, then, and Kitty's routines back up my own.

Certainly Kitty and I have got closer in the time we have lived together, but there is still a certain distance, which I sometimes regret, but, just as often, appreciate. She is still no "lap cat," but my sisters who have more experience than I do of pets, say that she will become just that as she gets older. And of course it would be so lovely if she would lie in my lap, although I don't want her to become too dependent on constant physical proximity. This would make it even more difficult for us to leave her by herself for a few days, and we do occasionally want to do that.

Even if Kitty does not lie in our laps, she has become more used to being handled. In the early days she grew stiff whenever we picked her up, but nowadays she is mostly fine with it. If I take her in my arms she usually purrs, and when we caress her she demonstratively lies down, purring, and turning herself belly-up. It looks almost indecent.

But sometimes she is keen to keep out of sight, and she does have her hiding places. Even if we know she is somewhere nearby she can be difficult to spot: a mattress under a bed in our guest room, and a Moses basket in which our children and grandchildren lay as newborns—now put away in a cramped attic—are two of the favorite places. Often we wonder how she has managed to get to the hidden places she loves. For instance, to get to the top shelf of our clothes rack in our utility room, she has to climb a vertical pole, balance on clothes hanging on a number of hangers, and crawl through a very narrow space between two of the bars forming the shelf on which we keep hats, gloves, and other things. Yet she makes her way up and down quite capably. Many of her favorite hangouts have one characteristic in common, namely that unless one makes a special effort, such as climbing onto a chair or ladder, it is not possible to know whether or not she's there. So she is usually left in peace, which is probably what she wants.

Yet, even though she sometimes withdraws herself, the level of trust between us is greater now than before. It has taken time. Cats do not take anything for granted.

Kitty's sense of security with us—and ours with her—has developed gradually, and there is still a note of estrangement. Still she can sometimes look frightened when we chance upon her unexpectedly, and I have never quite stopped anxiously asking myself whether she has disappeared forever, as soon as I have not seen her for a few hours. But over time we have come to trust one another more and more, and when we have not seen each other for a while she rubs her face against our legs and, as far as I can see, her only intention with this is to greet us. It has even become common for her to come when I whistle for her; maybe not immediately, but after a few minutes.

During the year or so that we have known each other, Kitty has not only had food and shelter. In becoming our house cat she has also had a career as a member of society—in a way only possible for cats.

In an organized country like Sweden, cats can be the subject of government enquiries. One's perspective on cats, these enquiries suggest, is dictated by their relationships to humans, which vary enormously. One extremity are the exclusive pedigree cats, costly products of a conscious breeding process that has made them into luxurious, decorative objects for their owners, who can even enter them into cat shows, winning money and prizes as a result. At the other end of the scale are the stray farm cats, cared for by no one and managing their own procreation with considerable success, without human intervention. Some of these strays have been abandoned or lost by accident, others are born wild by females that have no owners. Which of these alternatives apply to Kitty is something we will never know.

Seen from the perspective of the high-minded citizen, these stray cats are to be regarded as riffraff, almost the tramps of the animal kingdom, whose whereabouts can never be known with any certainty. Much like "these problematic members of society"—for that was how tramps were once viewed—they tend to breed quickly. Stray cats can present sanitary problems, they urinate and defecate in inappropriate places and their noisy sex lives, especially in spring nights, can disrupt sensitive people's sleep. As a result of their voracity, they can also contribute to the extinction of rare species of animals. And, the author of the study goes on, it's not enough to ensure that the cats are fed—their instincts drive them to hunt even when their bellies are full. Well thanks indeed for that, we're well aware of it! It's not hunger that makes our spoiled Kitty bring mice into the house at night.

Maybe the most upsetting thing of all is that the lumpenproletariat of the animal kingdom are in a bad way. Starving, sick cats are often so emaciated that their ribs stick out and their coats are full of fleas and lice. They pick up a range of diseases that can spread to other, better-cared-for cats and, in the worst-case scenario, to humans. Particularly in the case of intestinal parasites.

Any proper concern for people, the environment, and cats would seem to recommend the need for social intervention. It will not do to simply wait and see, experience shows that the population of stray cats is growing and consequently also is a problem.

Various solutions have been tried. One of these is a sort of public sterilization program: the cats are caught, castrated and then released. This approach has been adopted in certain locations in Denmark, for instance. Success has been moderate. For the population of stray cats to go down, at least three-quarters must be sterilized, which is not an easy proposition. There is also another genocidal approach, when strays are rounded up and exterminated. In Sweden we have a more cautious attitude. If the police capture a cat suspected of being a stray, the owners have ten days to get in contact. After the expiry of this period, the cat is the possession of the police, and subsequently is either sold or terminated. To conclude, a stray cat has absolutely no rights at all. Just imagine what a fate could have laid in store for Kitty if she had not conquered our hearts.

But nowadays Kitty has advanced herself to house-cat

status. She has a name and, like all proper cats, a chip with an identification code. The SVERAK register confirms that she belongs to us. She has also been spayed, a recommendation by the authorities for all cats that are allowed to run free.

Kitty is not even devoid of rights. She is our cat, we are responsible for her and if we neglect to give her the level of care that a cat needs, we could be in trouble with the authorities. By seducing us, Kitty may not have become a citizen, but she has been incorporated into Swedish society, with all the implications of how small or great animals must be treated. And more than that: she has become an exemplary cat, exactly the sort of cat that the solicitous authorities wish to have. Now we are only waiting for our "cat tax."

Kitty herself has changed since we became close. We feel that she has matured both physically and mentally. Not that she has lost her playfulness, she is just more grown-up and sure about her position. The half-grown, frozen, hungry cat that found an insecure haven in my gardening basket has developed into a self-confident house cat—a lady of certain habits. Sometimes it is almost as if she is confirming to herself with some satisfaction that her master and mistress have really been trained quite well, and are now behaving as people should toward a cat with certain expectations. And of course she's right. This is not only about us getting ourselves a cat; she has also found a pair of tame "cat people." We have—to our mutual satisfaction—tamed each other.

Physically also she has come a long way. Not that she has gained weight; she's a modest eater and has fully kept her youthful agility. It's true that nowadays she prefers to take a detour via a chair when jumping onto the kitchen counter where her food bowls are. But before you know it she'll be racing up a tree as quick as a flash, so there is absolutely nothing wrong with her vivacity. It's more laziness than excess weight that makes her opt for the chair. Why exert oneself needlessly?

Kitty has become a part of our lives, and vice versa. Not because we understand one another, but because we quite enjoy our time together. By now she is entirely dependent on the service we give her, and she keeps us going. We get a bit of exercise when we play with her, look for her, or try to get rid of the mice she brings in. And, not least important, we get a lot of laughs, which apparently prolongs one's life. Having someone to lavish one's care and attention on can be as important as receiving it from others.

For me, it has become a philosophical challenge to

try to understand at least a little about her world. She is after all a part of my daily social interaction and one likes to understand those who are close to one, even when they happen to be cats.

So we—the cat, the wife, and myself—expect to continue living together. It's a long-term commitment; cats can live for more than fifteen years. If I am still alive by then, I'll be going on ninety. I may never reach that sort of age. It's quite possible that Kitty will survive both me and my wife. There is something appealing about that. I wouldn't mind dying in my bed with Kitty somewhere close by. That is how friendly we have become. There was a cat at the old people's home where my mother spent her last days. She appreciated her very highly.